COLLECTED POEMS
OF
ELIZABETH BREWSTER

I

We acknowledge the support of the Canada Council for the
Arts, the Ontario Arts Council, the Government of Ontario
through the Ontario Media Development Corporation's
Book Publishing Tax Credit and Ontario Book Initiative
programs and the Government of Canada through the Book
Publishing Industry Development Program for our pub-
lishing activities.

ISBN 0 7780 1222 0 (hardcover)
ISBN 0 7780 1223 9 (softcover)

ONTARIO ARTS COUNCIL
CONSEIL DES ARTS DE L'ONTARIO

Cover art by Pablo Picasso
Book design by Michael Macklem

Printed in Canada

PUBLISHED IN CANADA BY OBERON PRESS

For Frances and Donald

Passage of Summer

Sunrise North

PASSAGE OF SUMMER

Past as Present

PAST AS PRESENT

I

Walking these streets so often walked before,
I almost feel as though my feet could find
Their former path, reach one familiar door
And enter to a world long left behind.

My father would be dozing with his pipe,
My mother in the kitchen baking bread.
I would sit down, warmed by the wood stove's fire,
And eat my evening supper with the dead.

The fried potatoes and the apple sauce,
The still warm loaf, the doughnuts sugared white
Would vanish from the table. Ancient jokes
Would circle ghostly in the encircling night.

II

If time's a mere delusion of the mind,
As the earth's fancied flatness tricks the eye,
Does not the whole scene stand as firm tonight
As once it seemed to stand? They did not die,

My parents, or that scene, then; no, nor scenes
Nor people who for ages seemed forgotten,
Indians whose bones here in the wilderness
Crumbled to dust, or flowers dank and rotten.

Those who drank hemlock or were crucified
Live in the triumph of their desolation.
Orpheus, though torn to death, remains untouched
To play his lute to a new generation.

The tastes of death and life are mixed together,
Honey and gall together on the tongue.
The newborn wither into dying age
While age renews its blossoms and is young.

RIVER SONG

Where are the lumberjacks who came from the woods for
    Christmas,
Drinking, fighting, singing their endless ballads,
Eating pork and pancakes for breakfast, gravy dripping over?
Where are their wives, milking the cows in winter,
Slopping out to the barn in rubber boots,
Shoveling out the snow drifts?
Churning, baking the crisp-scented bread in huge loaves?
Bearing their ten children?
Where is the shrill scream of the mill whistle,
The smell of a town built on sawdust and pine shavings?
Where are the logs afloat on the wide river?
Oh sad river,
Sing a song of pain for your children gone,
Oh glory gone.

THE IDIOT

The idiot with his slobbering mouth, half shoved,
Half led by his younger brother, slowly moved
Across my childhood's April. Stammering,
He handed me the violets of the spring,
And wished to please; but fright so sped my feet,
A timid child intolerant of the strange,
I dropped the flowers and ran, out of the range
Of slobber on petals blue and delicate.

Out of his range, in the white and wooden church,
I prayed, and felt my heart still work
Like churning butter. Why should an idiot
Be to the blossom like the blossom's rot?
My bowels turned that the ugly should be human,
That a boy should be like a white, unhealthy grub
Sliming the violets, yet be flesh and blood
And born to be a man from flesh of woman.

12

ORANGE ROOSTER

I remember in the farm yard
The orange rooster
With blue and green tail feathers
Shining like jewels,
And his handsome red comb,
And his operatic voice
Speaking of love.

How could he be expected
To be faithful to any one
Of those plain puritan
Plymouth Rock hens
Dressed in black and white
Unfashionable check?
But they followed adoring
His voice and his sheen,
Pecking each other
And waiting to be mounted.

13

SUNFLOWERS

My sister and I used to have contests
To see who could look longest at the sun.
We would stand in the centre of the green field
At full noon of summer,
Rooted in the ground like two sunflowers,
And stare up at that great round
Flame-coloured source of our life;
And when we closed our eyes a dozen suns
Danced on our darkened eyeballs.

Now I never look at the sun at all,
Except maybe when it rises or sets
Or is reflected in water
Shattered by waves.
My eyes will not endure
That burning joy.

14

MAKE-BELIEVE

The child, playing all day in the summer fields,
Was an Indian lying in a teepee with roof of timothy
And floor of vetch and clover; the smell of grass
Was sweet and hot and tickly in her nose.
Or, dressed in a straw hat and a blue sash,
She was the young Victoria in a portrait
Painted in childhood, princess blonde and good.
The Lake was the Sweet Thames, or it might be
Deerslayer's Lake, where Hutter had his home.
The growth of bush where blueberries darkly grew,
Spicy with ferns, was a woodchopper's forest
Where Hop-My-Thumb might wander;
And a deserted house in lonely fields
With broken windows and its walls unpainted
Was the bewitched tower where the lady slumbered
Through mouldering years, waiting a brown-eyed prince.

In dewy pastures steeds—not horses—whinnied;
Cows were bucolic in their patient ease;
And in the dim barn, smelling of hay and manure,
The barnyard cat with wizard yellow eyes,
Peering for mice, was lithe and gluttonous,
Cunning as any cat in ancient story.

15

POEM TO MY SISTER

Do you remember the houseboat that came and anchored
Out in the midst of the lake, one day in summer?
One of the boys rowed us out. We climbed on board,
And the skipper, old John Brown, showed us around.
"Just like a house," we said, and saw his kitchen,
With mugs and pancake flour stored on the shelf,
And his tidy bedroom with his bunk and books.

And always after that we envied him—
I did at least—able to drop his anchor
Out there on the Lake and look across the water
At ordinary householders on shore.
It must have been like living on an island
In a world separate as a rounded shell.
Water lapped him to sleep and dawn awoke him.
The fibrous yellow lilies floated near,
And trees along the shore cast green reflections.
The daytime sun was lazy on the ripples,
And in the evening all the farmhouse lights
Glinted like warmer stars fallen from the skies.
Perhaps those houses seemed enchanted too
To one who watched their lights shine on the water
And wondered who had lit the yellow lamps
Or stood beside the windows looking out.

STAR BRIGHT

I remember a night of childhood in late August
Going home from a picnic. There were, I think,
Six or so of us in an old wagon.
The horse clop-clopped along the dusty road.
I made a wish, I remember, on the first star,
And then we sat and tried to count the stars.
It might have taken as long, we thought, to count them
As to count the pebbles lying on the road
That seemed the stars' reflections. They seemed so far,
Untouched by any sentimental song
Or speculations of astronomers.
We sang a while, until the shadowy trees
And the calm moonlight stilled the song to rest;
Then huddled closer, like young animals
That warm each other in the cool of night.

I wonder what my wish was on the star:
Maybe for riches, like the girl whose apron
Was filled with falling stars that turned to coins;
Maybe for glory, like a crown of stars;
Maybe to travel far and far away,
Where different constellations burned in air;
Maybe for love to turn my blood to stars.
I can't somehow remember, but I wish—
Or half wish, maybe—I could find myself
On a calm August evening in a creaking wagon
Driving home between the rows of pines.

THE NIGHT GRANDMA DIED

"Here's Grandmother in here," Cousin Joy said,
Standing beside me at the bedroom door,
One hand on my shoulder. "You see, she's only sleeping."
But I, nine years old and frightened,
Knew it was a lie. Grandmother's shell
Lay on the bed, hands folded, head on one side,
The spirit that had groaned so loud an hour ago
Gone out of her. I looked, and turned and ran,
First to the kitchen. There were the aunts
Who had laid her out, still weeping
Over a good hot cup of tea: Aunt Stella,
Large, dominant; Aunt Alice, a plump, ruffled hen of a woman;
My small, quick mother; Aunt Grace, youngest and shyest,
Awkward on the edge of the group: "Shush," she was saying
To Cousin Pauline, who was lying on the floor
Pretending to be Grandma.

And they all got up and came into the parlour,
Where suddenly everyone was jovial,
And Aunt April sat in the best chair
Nursing her newest baby,
And the uncles sat talking of crops and weather,
And Uncle Harry, who had come from Maine,
Pumped the hands of people he hadn't seen in twenty years,
And Grandma's nephew Eb from up the road
Played everybody's favourite tune on the piano.
Now and then, remembering the corpse, he burst into a
    Baptist hymn,
His rich bass voice, dark and deep as molasses,
Flowing protectively over the women,
While his eyes, also dark,
Wrapped them warm with sympathy.

18

And I, sitting on a footstool in a corner,
Was sometimes warmed by the voice,
And sometimes chilled remembering
In the room next door
Grandmother, dead, whom I had never liked.

SILENCE IS OBSOLETE

Silence is obsolete, that thick silence
Soft as snow or a slow bird's wing
Spread over the world, which I remember
From the days of a farm childhood
When cars did not run on the winter roads
And we sat in the snow-dark house
Without radio or television or telephone
In a family not given to chat,
Each wrapped around in the folds of his own thought,
Deep and thick as wool.

Awakening to the roar of Hondas
Or my neighbour playing his transistor in the bath
Through the too-thin walls of the apartment building,
I regret that we have abolished silence.
Now, although we may perhaps be lonely,
We are never really alone,
And therefore never perfectly together.

19

IN THE VENUS RESTAURANT

Sitting opposite these two young persons,
Male and female,
Who are eating chips in a booth
And are both wearing tight pants,
Leather jackets, and long straight hair,
I try to imagine myself at the same age
Sitting with them and thinking their thoughts;
And I remember myself in my 'teens,
Very thin, in a yellow dirndl skirt with red flowers,
Disliking the short skirt because of my bow legs,
Wearing white bobby socks and dirty sneakers
And going for long walks by myself.

And I remember once walking
Past a tennis court where a boy and girl in white,
My supposed contemporaries,
Were playing together,
Looking like an ad for Coca-Cola.
I watched them with envy and contempt,
And was further away from them, I think now,
Than the distance of the gap of generations
Between myself and these two young persons,
Who, after all, look as messy as I did.

STARLINGS

I remember one autumn
There was a surplus of starlings,
And they used to shoot them
In the early morning.
Later, walking through the campus,
We stumbled on dead starlings,
Heaped up feathered bodies.
Somebody told me it must have been a dream,
One of those nightmares one has
On hot dark nights:
They wouldn't have let all those birds lie rotting.
But it wasn't a dream.
I was there.

21

TO HOMAI

Two years ago we sat in a Roman theatre
On the edge of an English city. Weeds and grass
Grew over the stone seats and around them.
In a field near by a child was picking poppies
Waist-high in grass. The quiet was so deep
The tender stems seemed to make a sound in snapping.

And as we talked and ate stale buns from London
We wondered how they felt, those Romans, in their day,
When, foreigners as we were, they sat where we sat,
Thinking, perhaps, of home, or eyeing the local girls,
Or merely wondering if there'd be a rain.

Why were they here, under these soft, low skies
Instead of in Italy's distant bluenesses?
Wondering, we asked. Would someone wonder too
About us in the years that were to come?

But then you shook the crumbs off from your sari
And said we should be catching the next 'bus,
And that was that, for us and for the Romans.

Now on what strange and distant Himalayas
Do your eyes touch, though I shall never know them?
And will you ever see
This small, particular stretch of summer sky,
Its hot blue tongue licking the ice cream clouds?
Are you nearer to me than those dead Romans were
We talked of on a summer afternoon
Two years and several thousand lives ago?

IN THE LIBRARY

Believe me, I say to the gentleman with the pince-nez,
Framed forever with one hand in his pocket,
With passion, with intensity I say it—
Believe me, oh believe me, you are not I.
Making my chair squeak on the chilly floor,
Catching up my pencil, I say—
But of course I am myself.

And all the while time flows, time flows, time flows;
The minutes ripple over the varnished tables.
This is June, I say, not yesterday or tomorrow.
This is I, not Byron or Vanessa. I am not in the moon.
I must differentiate my body from all other bodies,
Realizing the mole on my neck, the scar on my hand.
I must wind my watch, say it is ten o'clock.
But I know I am not convinced, feel uneasily the lie.
Because actually I am Byron, I am Vanessa,
I am the pictured man with the frigid smile.

I am the girl at the next table, raising vague eyes,
Flicking the ash from her cigarette, the thoughts from her
    mind.
The elastic moment stretches to infinity,
The elastic moment, the elastic point of space.
The blessed sun becomes the blessed moon.

23

ALONE IN THE PUBLIC ROOM

Alone in the public room
Listening to retreating footsteps
Listening to a whistle and a scrap of song,
I, who must always tiptoe over floors,
Stand with raised hand and thudding heart outside doorways,
Linger embarrassed in the corridors of life,
Apologizing, back out of rooms like an intruder—
I, who listen too nervously to the epoch-shattering stroke of
    the clock
I would imitate, if I could, the staccato, assured footsteps,
The whistle unconscious of fear, scornful of time.
But is it worth it? I ask, Is it worth it?
And think more respectfully of the fox's sincerity.

24

ALONE IN HOTEL BEDROOM

I sit on the edge of a bed with a pink bedspread
And face the wall with a mirror, the green dressing table.
The other walls are blank, excepting
For the two anonymous bird pictures.
There are two green armchairs and a television
And a window overlooking a public square.
The advertising sign for Central Trust
Winks on and off below me,
And if I stand up I can see the cars
Crawling down the hill of the grey street;
Or, lying back, I hear them roaring past
Unendingly, like a long funeral.

Shut in by these four walls, I am alone
As a hermit on a pillar in the desert.
Surely now, I think, I can find some meaning
Which eludes me in the daily passage of time,
Piling the breakfast dishes in the sink,
Listening to the news on the transistor,
Locking and unlocking office doors,
Listening with sympathy, or pretended sympathy,
To accounts of quarrels, funerals, sicknesses,
Turning the pages of old books and new books
And copying out the information on their title pages
Carefully, with concern for commas,
Arguing with a neighbour about the need for fluoridation.

And do I care about the teeth of future generations?
Or how many there are in future generations?
And if their numbers are controlled by birth control,
Or bombs, or famine?
Do I disapprove of euthanasia?
Am I, or am I not, a good Catholic?
Have I ever been in love?
Do I believe in being in love?
Do I believe in being?

In Grade Eight I walked to school
With a school bag on my shoulder
Wondering if I really existed
And if the school bag was real.
And in high school I read Plato
Attempting to prove immortality
And for the first time doubted immortality.
I wanted to be clever like Socrates
And question everything,
All our patriotic ideals and our gods
And our inherited virtues.
I wanted to exasperate people
And to prove they were all foolish except me.

And yet I woke up in the night
Praying for a God to pray to,
And envied the faith of mad old Tom,
Who, after a Roller meeting,
Made himself wings
And jumped off the barn roof,
Thinking God would hold him up.
Even though he broke his ankle,
He still managed to keep his faith.

And I admired the goodness
Of the old man whose black suits were green
Because, in the days of the Depression,
He lived on half his income
And gave the rest to his neighbours.
I could not imagine liking money so little.

Now the darkness is deep outside.
A thunder storm has come and gone.
Cars still drive through the wet streets.
Wrapping a blanket around me,
I sit dreaming,
Knowing I do not expect
To make up my mind
Once and for all
On any great question,
Tonight or any night.

Tomorrow, I remember, is Pascal's birthday
Puritan and gambler
On the game of faith.
And I remember
The girl in my office
Who plays bingo every Tuesday.
"Some people always win," she says,
"But me—I always lose.
But I go all the same."

WHAT I WANT IS STONE

What I want is stone:
Rocks so old they can never be volcanic,
Worn down, smooth,
Free of grass, moss, the clambering violet.
Atoms may dance in them a little,
Since all atoms dance,
But a staid, invisible measure,
Not fire, not flux,
Not waves
Of mutability.

The world moves too fast
For my middle age.
I do not like
People marching with placards
Or covering themselves with pitch
And setting fire to themselves.
The mean is my ideal,
The eighteenth century
(Which I suppose never really existed)
With grave, solid, expensive buildings,
Classical, sober, in good taste,
Not extravagant Gothic
Yearning to heaven
Or fussy, cozy Victorian
Idolizing the hearth
Or the too dramatic
Show-off twentieth century.

28

I want to open a new novel
And find it was written by Jane Austen.
Civilization should tame barbarism,
Decorum should control passion,
The will subdue the act.
Humanity should be a statue
Senatorial, calm, with a Roman smile
Ironic, wise, malicious, and Augustan.

What I want is stone.

Dream Landscape

THE CAVE

I remember, when I was a child, there was a cave
Not far from the house. I often played
Beside its mouth, and, gazing
Into its black depths, wondered where it led.
There might be some old pirate's treasure hidden,
A chest of rubies in an inner room;
Or perhaps it was a room for skulls and ghosts,
Or a passage leading by intricate paths and byways
To the grim fastnesses of Giant Despair.
Should I go in? All fairyland might greet me,
My godmother mounted on a pumpkin coach
To lead me to the throne room of the Prince,
Strewing my path with primroses and diamonds.
But what if the godmother were a wicked witch?
I might be frozen to an icicle,
Hung mesmerized from the ceiling of the cave,
Like a foolish, dangling, suicidal corpse.
I stood and stared and wavered, wondering,
But feared too much to step inside the door.

So I stand still before the cave of the soul
Fearing some well, some quicksand,
Some treachery in the paths,
The violence of the Furies who inhabit
The depths below and cry aloud for vengeance.
I need some password or some secret sign
To guide me through these chambers where strange figures
Stare at me dimly from the carven walls;
Some magic food to eat
Until I reach that safe, interior room
Where the Prince sits in serene majesty
Waiting to greet me with his golden ring
And lead me to his solemn banquet table.

DREAM LANDSCAPE

What is this dark landscape of my dreams,
These paths where it is always hard walking,
In country lanes or on some city side street,
A dark alley lined by crowded tenements?
What are the scuffles in the dark, the muted violence?
What are the bridges that are so hard to cross?
What are the rooms I walk through, the empty corridors
Hollowly echoing to uncertain feet,
The unfurnished apartments always to be let,
The dining rooms where meals are never served?

What are these crowds gathered to see a play—
Comedy or tragedy, nobody knows which—
Where the blonde and beautiful heroine weeps and smiles?
Or are they waiting for a symphony to begin
While the instruments tune up but never play?

And what is the name of this grey, restless sea
By which I walk, escaped from crowds and houses?
How beautiful and perilous the path
Along the rocky coast, watching the gulls dip
From a patch of lonely sky, watching the spray
Tossed high by the wind against the waiting rocks.
What are these rocks? What is this tossing spray?

IF I COULD ESCAPE

If I could escape from all the walls and rooms
That hold me back, escape from all the streets
If I could escape from time, from the morning alarm clock,
If I could go free into another spring time,
And smell the sensuous light smell of lilacs,
And see them rising like a purple smoke;
If I could be the wind blowing through the lilacs,
Now soft and aching, with fingers on their hair
Delicate and compassionate as the touch of love,
Now fierce and free, piling the frightened clouds
Into a mounded frenzy in mid-air,
Scattering the blossoms, flinging branches to earth;

If I could lie with my face against the ground
Like a swimmer swimming through green waves of grass
And clover like white foam, bathed in green light,
Smelling the steamy sweetness of the earth;
Oh, if I could escape and run, and run
Across the unfenced fields, or into the woods
Where no one ever comes, tangled and deep,
If I could break the doors and smash the windows
And bribe the angel with the flaming sword
Who guards the Eden of my lost desires
To let me past the gate, I'd never come back,
But camp like a gypsy in the wilderness
And live on honey and wild blackberries.

IF I COULD WALK OUT INTO
THE COLD COUNTRY

If I could walk out into the cold country
And see the white and innocent dawn arise:
The mist stealing away, leaving the low hills
Bathed in pale light; the pink, unreal sun;
The jagged trees stabbing the cold, bright sky;
If I could walk over stubble fields white with frost
And see each separate small beaded blade
Loaded and edged with white; or climb the fence
Of grey and twisted wood, to find and eat
The crab-apples in the pasture, sharp with frost;
If I could shelter, shivering in a clump of woods
To watch the chill and beautiful day go past;
Perhaps I might find again my lost childhood,
A ghost blowing with the November wind,
Or buried in the wood, like those dead pioneers
Whose tumbled tombstones I found overgrown with
    brambles,
Their names erased, in an unfrequented way.

CHILD'S DREAM

In her dream the child was playing with her friends
A happy game of tag with outstretched hands.
Innocent as sunshine they were dancing
And touched her with the softness of spring winds.

And then in the midst of all their joyful prancing
She saw they were lions on their prey advancing,
And she was running from their muscular power
And the darkness of their shadows forward lunging.

They followed her, tongues dripping to devour.
Their evil jaws, all wet with foam and gore,
Worked up and down. Could she ever now be sure
That they'd been innocent children just before?

35

The princess wore her hair long. Yellow as butter,
It fell to her waist, as straight as any mermaid's.
Her dress was blue, to tranquillize the monster.
For years he had eaten a virgin every year,
Perhaps a raft of virgins; but now, grown old,
He might be growing milder. He lay in bed,
His grizzled bear's head propped against the pillows,
And smiled at her benignly. In her hand
She held a cup, filled with the magic gruel.
He drank it up, except for one last drop,
Then asked for water to wash that drop down.
That was a trick, she knew. She must refuse him,
Or else her death would follow. She refused.

The gruel, she said, must always be made fresh.
Water would ruin it. He nodded gravely.
And could she make some fresh? Oh, yes, she could,
But it would take a while. She must wander far;
The ingredients were hard, at times, to come by.
You could find moss in the woods, and crimson berries
Picked by the edge of a spring. You needed those.
Oh, but it was a secret recipe.

And could she go to pick them? The window was open
And she looked out and saw the lilac in bloom,
And the white clouds dreamily blown across the sky,
And one free bird wheeling and circling above.
Perhaps, he said, his eyes pursuing hers,
Perhaps I'll let you go, and I'll go too.

TWO DREAMS: II

When we moved into the Fortress it was night.
The landlady said we really ought to wait.
There was no furniture; the place was in need of repair;
All the buildings were falling down except that one,
And it was old, but it would keep the rain out.
It would be a shelter, if we had nowhere to stay,
And we were welcome to it. So we moved in.

Afterwards it seemed better than we had thought.
The wood of the long hall was heavy and solid,
Dark with the passage of years, carved in strange shapes
The fireplace welcomed us. We knelt before it,
Warming our fingers. So we settled down.

When morning came we discovered it was June.
Flinging the window open I stood and gazed
And called, "Come here, come here, look at the garden."
We looked down at the courtyard, green and blossoming,
Ranged in a tidy square. Around the fountain
Children were dancing. There was never such fragrance and
   freshness.

They came out then from the neighbouring houses to greet us.
There were floats and banners and a long procession.
In the centre of the courtyard a girl was dancing.
The children clapped their hands. The procession stood still,
And from their hands and the hands of women on doorsteps
Petals floated. The trees shook down their petals.
And as we stood and watched her from our window
Her small white feet seemed petals dancing.

DREAM

I dreamed that I was buried live.
My spirit took a spade
And dug the earth where deep
My body had been laid.

If I arrived in time
I knew I had a spark
Would light my fainting life,
Even in that dark.

But when my spade had struck
The coffin, I was dead,
Body and silent heart.
Only my severed head

Cut from my naked neck,
Still lived, and faintly spoke
With senseless, twittering tongue.
Its eyes, with clouded look,
Stared at me and implored
My help by deed or word.

38

CAT

Last night, in the hot, moist night,
I thought I was wakened
When a huge cat
With thick yellow fur
And yellow eyes
Thudded on my bed.
But it was only the heat of the night,
Thick and smothering
As cat fur.

REALITY AS ESCAPE

It is not in dreams
That we escape.
Reality protects
Against reality.
We are reassured by
Forms made in quadruplicate
Letters piled on the desk
Pounding of typewriters
Coffee break coke break
Juke boxes wailing
Breakfast dinner supper lunch breakfast
Can openers opening cans
The Sunday roast
Lectures on the nature of poetry
Forums on the nature of students
TV radio record-player telephone
The visiting violinist
The hairdresser the barber
The corner shop the supermarket
The daily paper the monthly magazine
The debate in the Commons, the row in the Town Council
The children playing in the back yard—
All the variety of daily living.

It is only in dreams
When we are alone
That the terror behind life
Rises from the depths:
The dark monsters of nightmare
And the glaring lights
Of explosive war,
Able to melt eyeballs
From useless sockets
As we go wandering
In search of death.

SHELTER

I dreamed I was spending Christmas
In an air raid shelter
With my father and the president
Of the local Catholic Women's League.
Germany had bombed Greece,
Or maybe Greece had bombed Germany,
But anyhow the world outside
Was wrecked. There were Visigoths
Marching in the streets of Rome;
Desert sand blew around
One white ruined column
On the banks of the Nile;
And on abandoned farms
Just outside our shelter
The farm dogs hunted
In packs like wolves.
Their siren howls
Distracted us from trimming
Our Christmas tree.

HAUNTING

In my dream
I seem to awaken.
My mother is in the kitchen
Making coffee for someone.
I hear their voices
And go out in my dressing gown
To see who is there.
It is my father
Wrapped in flames
Like the ghost of Hamlet's father.
"Don't be afraid," my mother
Says. "It's just Purgatory
He's been in. He's been resting
Over the North Star."

Tears run down my cheeks
As I put my arms around him
In the flames.
"Oh, my dear," I say,
"I am in Purgatory too.
Help me."

42

STAIRWAY

When I was a child
Walking up and down a stairway
I stepped in a certain way
On a certain step
And thought all my future
And the future of the world
Appeared in a vision
And vanished instantly.
Afterwards I could not remember
What I saw.
For many days
I walked up and down the steps,
Hoping to find the right one,
But that was the only vision
I ever had.

43

COUNTRY CELLAR

Down
    Down
        Down
            the steps
To the dark cellar
Damp and ground smelling
Cool in the heat of midsummer
Where the cream sits in cans
And in the wooden shelves along the wall
Are rows and rows of jam jars
Full of the dark red
Sugar sweet
Preserved berries.

I dreamed a dream
In which my love grew sick
From the taste of berries
Because they tasted too much
Of the earth.

ADRIFT

We were adrift in a boat
Without sail, oars, or engine
On a green, rolling sea.
A clown tried to distract us
From our terror
With his painted cheeks and putty nose,
Bauble rattling in hand.
We would not be distracted.
Salt water
Blew up and
Lashed over our faces.
When I awoke
I could still taste salt
On my lips.

45

On Considering Objects

ON CONSIDERING OBJECTS

I remember an old lady who once said to me,
"Why are young persons bored? If you are bored,
Consider the object nearest you,
Whether it's the geranium on your window sill,
Or a cup, or a glass, or a box of matches.
Do you understand it thoroughly?
Could you make it?
If you understand it,
Then you are a scientist
And a philosopher.
If you can make it,
You have a craft or at least a hobby.
If you can do neither,
Admire the skill of God or your fellow labourer,
And recognize your own ignorance."

And so I sit this morning
Watching a fly which has landed
And is crawling laboriously
On the edge of the flowered sugar bowl
Half full of white, shining sweet crystals.

BUD VASE

My neighbour has cut me these roses,
Two buds on one stem,
So perfect, so tightly gathered at the centre
In untouched silken folds of dusky red,
Rising so tranquilly
From evenly notched clusters of green leaves,
And breathing so faintly
A scent as dim as strawberry blossoms
That I almost think
They must be manufactured
Waxen blossoms with applied perfumes.
Only I see one solitary petal
Delicately cut, as though tooth marked:
By weather, or the authenticating mark
Of the hungry, not-to-be-deceived,
Fastidious
Worm?

PET SNAKE

This grass-green grass snake,
Beautiful as grass,
Is tired, naturally,
Having just shed his skin.
He is the children's pet,
Who love his ripples,
Sinuous as waves,
Who force-feed him with frogs
To keep him bright
As emerald
And to make his eyes shine, also jewel-like.
His small tongue
Is delicate and supple
As himself.
To own him is to own
A patch of jungle
Ancient and wild as time.

48

JENNIFER

Jennifer has a number of likes:
Pigeons, for instance,
And frogs, and snakes,
And wild roses on the beach,
And waves with whitecaps,
And the boats on the water,
Which she calls chugboats;
And she can spend a lot of time
Quite happily
Listening to the sound
Her loose tooth makes
When she pushes it back and forth.
She can, if necessary,
Tolerate her brothers,
And plays marbles with them.
Last, and especially,
She likes driving home through
Fireflies shining
In the pinch-black night.

49

WALKERS

There is a child walking,
Head up, swinging his arms,
Courageous in this so-big world
Where distances appal.
His life is all morning,
A glorious time for catching ladybugs.
Sounds sharp as pebbles
Rattle against his ears,
And all light is jagged
Like summer lightning.

There is a young girl walking,
Mincing on too-high heels,
Conscious of her own selfhood,
Her body like a swaying plant.

The celluloid caresses of film stars
Mingle in her mind
With the languorous grace of
Elaine and Guinevere.

There is an old man walking
With shuffling steps,
Tottering a little
Under the weight of years.
His eyes are china-blue,
Faded with many suns.
Layers of childhood swim
Beneath their surface.

ATLANTIC DEVELOPMENT

Three abandoned churches in a row;
Tombstones behind them hidden by waving timothy;
A farmhouse with broken panes,
Still shielded by limp curtains, dark with dust;
Further along the road, a deserted mineshaft.
In the neighbouring village
The only young men on the street are these granite soldiers
Carved on the war memorial in front of the Post Office.

THE MOON IS A MIGHTY MAGNET

The moon is a mighty magnet. It draws
With all its force
The foaming tides
Up the long reaches
Of the shore.
Also it raises the tides of blood and life
In menstruous women
Twisting their bowels and bellies.

It draws desire,
Although it has falsely been called
Diana's bow, the bow of chastity.
Lunatics, it is said,
Are made restless by its changes—
Not just Elizabethan lunatics
But our own less beautifully named
"Mentally ill," in their inspected institutions.

I know a little boy
Who loves magnets,
Keeps them in his pocket,
Makes houses and worlds with them.
I think what he would most like for a birthday present
Is the moon in his pocket. For why?
Because the moon is a mighty magnet.

The moon draws so many things:
Now it is drawing men.
They are drawn up
Like nails or needles
In their metal space capsules.
Soon they will reach the moon,
Explore its hollows and crevices,
Mountains, craters.

And will those feet
Plonk-plonk along
The silent silver pastures
Of the moon?

52

BEYOND OUTER SPACE

Though astronauts may anchor
In harbours of the moon
Or pioneer the planets
That swing about the sun;

Though stars be mapped and charted
To the dim edge of night
Until the world of darkness
Clamps down on farther flight;

Yet past the farthest boundaries
Still other worlds find place
And burning unknown planets
Flame beyond time or space.

Here when the mind needs deserts
She still can find a home
Where fields are wide and lonely
And only thought can come.

53

NOTHING IS LIKE NOTHING ELSE

When I was young and knew no better
I was always wanting to compare this to that:
Hearts might be cold as ice cream cones;
Water shone like flashlights;
Autumn leaves were mustard
On the sky's blue china plate.

But now I know different.
Now I know that nothing is like nothing else.
A white plate is a white plate, smooth, glossy;
Snow is another whiteness: not powdery,
Not like wool or silk or feathers,
But like itself, cold, dense, soft,
And yet sometimes hard, sometimes pointed,
Reflecting the sky, which is not like blue nylon,
But has its own special colour, texture, absence of texture.
And there are so many objects,
So many whites, blues, transparencies,
That the eye and the mind must be careful,
Must work very hard not to be confused by them.

And when I get beyond objects
(Seashells, mirrors, bottles of ginger ale,
Daisy petals, and all the rest)
And try to consider minds and motives
And poetry and politics
And work and friendship—
Then language is difficult indeed,
Since minds are never alike
And never like snow.

THE CHILD WITH ALICE HAIR

The child with Alice hair
Yearning for LSD
Or marijuana
Feels the old Faustian urge
For forbidden apples
On a forbidden tree:

To know all, to be all,
To collect experience up
In a cup of thrills,
To taste strange lusts,
Perverted lechery,
And yet to be a mediaeval nun
As cold as charity
Posed in a photograph
On the dew-fringed lawn
Of an invented convent;

Not to be limited,
Not to be one,
This one human person
Living one life
Watching from a single window
The tree across the way
Gradually put forth leaves
Which flourish, which wither,
Which fall, to live again;

This one person, who cannot imagine
The whole human race,
But sees only
The neighbour child
Crossing the street
With his pet turtle.

GREEN PASTURES

I sometimes envy my friend who studies shellfish,
Ignoring those other specimens, the fishermen,
Who no doubt think her cuckoo
To be wandering about the shores at such odd hours.
Other times she teaches her students to dissect cats
Or to observe the embryos of chicks.
These are definite realities, to be described definitely.

Or I envy my neighbour,
Whose painting of bathers diving
Into green waves
Patterns their motion.
Here too there is clarity,
A sharp definition of edges.

Or I envy the philosophy professor
Who, having tried the field glasses of a dozen philosophies—
None true, for what is truth?—
Can see the world through the total
Of their wrong ends,
Safe and diminished.

But a poem is not as definite as a diagram,
Obtains its colour only by pretence,
So that if I were to try to put this room into a poem
I could not really make you see
The untidy desk with open drawers;
The typewriter, paper, books on top of it;
The kitchen chair with a sweater over its back;
The red rug slightly awry, the dust on the dresser,
The clutter of combs, perfume, penny bank, scissors;
An aspirin and a vitamin pill side by side;
The bed where I sit writing, propped against pillows.

And if I did manage to make you see the room,
I do not think I could show any truth behind it,
Anything that would make this room
Signify other than just being a room
Where somebody sometimes lives, and types, and sleeps.

CONVERSATION CONTINUED

What you say about one experience
Equalling another is perhaps true.
X+y does tend to balance a−b.
Spending one's childhood in a debtors' prison
Equals, perhaps, being the dilettante son
Of a Prime Minister, and able to afford
Friendships with poets or a Gothic castle.
Proust in his cork lined room, Thoreau at Walden
Each knew a different face of solitude.
Crossing the Atlantic in an immigrant vessel
Might not be as adventurous
As taking a walking tour through Wales
Or travelling by coach from Steventon to Bath.
A spinster in New England or Yorkshire
Writing of an imaginary lover
Might be as close to reality
As the young man from Ayrshire
Singing of his Mary, Jean, Clarinda, and etcetera,
Since love may be known in some ways from its absence
As well as from its presence,
And St. Teresa's darts, flames, and sighs
Are as hot and piercing
As any other lover's.

Portraits

HOME FOR THE AGED

The old men sit, five of them on a bench,
Half sleeping, half awake, dazed by the sun,
In the muted afternoon, between one broadcast ball game and
  the next.
Their thoughts are leaves that drift across a sky perpetually
  autumn.
Their hands are folded: they have done with the Sunday papers.
Decorously shabby, decently combed and clean,
They watch with half-closed eyes the passers-by,
The loitering lovers, the boys on bikes, the cars
Rushing eagerly to some scene of active life.

Their lives are folded up like the papers, and who can know
Whether their years passed sober and discreet,
With the measured, dutiful, regular click of a clock,
Or whether some old violence lingers still
In faded headlines on their dusty brains?
What boyhood do they wander in, what middle age forget?
And do they watch their dwindling stock of time
With hope, or resignation, or despair?

58

GREAT-AUNT REBECCA

I remember my mother's Aunt Rebecca
Who remembered very well Confederation
And what a time of mourning it was.
She remembered the days before the railway,
And how when the first train came through
Everybody got on and visited it,
Scraping off their shoes first
So as not to dirty the carriage.
She remembered the remoteness, the long walks between
  neighbours.
Her own mother had died young, in childbirth,
But she had lived till her eighties,
Had borne eleven children,
Managed to raise nine of them,
In spite of scarlet fever.
She had clothed them with the work of her own fingers,
Wool from her own sheep, spun at home,
Woven at home, sewed at home
Without benefit of machine.
She had fed them with pancakes and salt pork
And cakes sweetened with maple sugar.
She had taught them one by one to memorize
"The chief end of man is to know God,"
And she had also taught them to make porridge
And the right way of lighting a wood fire,
Had told the boys to be kind and courageous
And the girls never to raise their voices
Or argue with their husbands.

59

I remember her as an old woman,
Rheumatic, with folded hands,
In a rocking chair in a corner of the living room,
Bullied (for her own good) by one of her daughters.
She marveled a little, gently and politely,
At radios, cars, telephones;

But really they were not as present to her
As the world of her prime, the farmhouse
In the midst of woods, the hayfields
Where her husband and the boys swung their scythes
Through the burning afternoon, until she called for supper.

For me also, the visiting child, she made that world more real
Than the present could be. I too
Wished to be a pioneer,
To walk on snowshoes through remote pastures,
To live away from settlements an independent life
With a few loved people only; to be like Aunt Rebecca,
Soft as silk and tough as that thin wire
They use for snaring rabbits.

60

LADY IN A SMALL TOWN

Delicate as the soufflés that she makes
To serve to guests in her small, virginal room,
She's all gentility, a portrait suited
To this elaborate Victorian frame:

The ornate clock, the china animals,
The inherited, masculine books, the spindly chairs,
The photographs of college presidents,
Her father and grandfather, whose dead stares

Still awe her. Cranford seems her home.
This village is not Cranford, though. The wind
Blows here so constantly the trees all grow
A little crooked from it. Even in this room
You feel the house shake when the marsh winds blow,
And, brave as any tree, you see her bend.

JANE

A notable housewife in her time was Jane.
In her small parlour every object stood
Frozen to stillness, as though under glass,
Dustless as though no gust of summer air
Ever blew dust from the brown road outside.
The china ornaments, the upright books
Standing like soldiers never put at ease
(No dog-eared novel flung at random down
On floor or sofa, but, sternly upright,
Livingstone's Journeys or a book of sermons),
The tidy pictures never hung awry,
The clock which, ticking, scarcely seemed to tick,
The desk not marred by any cluttered papers,
Ash trays where ashes never dared to fall,
The decorous chairs which knew their place and kept it—
All these were shining with their mistress' care.

She had been married, but in time her husband,
A meek, apologetic man who padded
About the house in slippers, faded away
To live his separate and untidy life
In a cabin in the woods. Now both are dead,
Husband and married spinster, and the house
Sold to another family.
                              They had one son,
A neat boy also, licked to perfect shape.
His wife, they say, is a good housewife too.

ANNA

Anna, being the eldest of nine children,
Had always much to do about the house,
But, being stronger than most girls, was ready
To help her father plough or cut the firewood.
Her body was clumsy, but her bony hands
Were light and kind with babies or with horses.

She married, when she was no longer young,
A widower with five sons. She thought him kind,
Though sometimes wishing, when he snored beside her
For the swaggering lumberjack whose dancing eyes
Had awed her tongue-tied girlhood. When she woke
And lit the lamp for breakfast, all her mind
Turned to her day's work, to the milking and baking,
Washing and ironing. She had little time
For rest, except nights when she mended
And thought with half her mind; or cool June evenings
When walking through the hayfields in the dusk
She smelled the summer round her; or the Sundays
She went to meeting in her one good dress
And, kneeling with the parson's voice above her
Like a fly buzzing somewhere in a corner,
Thanked God she had been luckier than most.

PAPER FLOWERS

Cousin Josephine made paper flowers,
Sitting in the winter by the kitchen fire
With crepe paper and wire stems on the stand beside her.
"You look real summery in here," visitors would say.
But in the summer she made them just the same,
Perched on the stiff-backed love seat in the parlour
Under the portrait of Lord Kitchener in regimentals.
The shades were drawn to keep out the July sun
And the windows closed to keep out the scent of the garden.
Her snipping scissors whistled above the grasshoppers' song,
Cutting through yards and yards of crinkled paper.
The house was full of false flowers, spilling from bulging vases
And lying in tangled heaps on the tops of desks.
And when she died, one snowy day in April,
They piled her coffin high
With paper lilies and waxed daffodils.

64

LOUISA

Louisa, who, before her wedding day
Had dreamed of rural peace, Arcadian bliss,
Life ripening calmly in a country village,
Found herself, after twenty years, despising
Her good dull husband and his good dull town.
There was no escape, none, from the coffin walls
Of her house closing round her, or the warm breath
And peering, inquisitive faces of too-close neighbours.
In vain she went for walks: the clouds were curdled,
And dust was white and thick on every leaf.
She counted the same pebbles every time.
In vain she pulled the shades, to make within
A little island of her room, playing her records,
A trickle of aimless sound teasing her ears.
She sickened without reason, found herself
Too wearied out to dress or comb her hair,
And lay all day upon her unmade bed.

When the young doctor came, she found life brighter.
She discovered her lipstick again, a forgotten dimple;
Put on her prettiest dressing gown, and served him
Pale china tea in her most delicate cups.
His sympathy was sweet: he too was an outsider,
Banded with her against an alien world.
Candid and young, he was the son she lacked,
The husband she had wanted. Being neither,
He still could be her lover. So he was.

When he married, her cardboard happiness toppled down.
Her jealous fancy played with knives and poison
Or built up scenes in which she pleaded with him,
Recalling similes of stones and ice.
She wrote him letters, amorous or threatening,
And watched his house to see him go or come.

65

Weary, perhaps afraid, he moved from town.
Alone with her husband, she wept, was conscience-stricken,
Returned to religion, prayed and wept again;
Knelt in a feverish transport of devotion;
But, whispering "Bless me, Father," felt unblessed;
Absolved, was not absolved; played with good works
And gave them up again; at length retreated
To the stale desolation of her sickness,
The chosen Waste Land of her living room.

PROBLEM CHILD

What is there in the boy
That foils his parents' or his teachers' breath?
Politely listening, he turns aside
Their scoldings' blunted edge.

He moves like air or water round their wills,
That seems to yield but closes up behind.
They lecture him: his face is like his mind,
Wears on its surface a close-buttoned smile.

Ambiguously, they do not know themselves
Why they must batter down his last retreat.
They hope they want to help him, but are baffled
By his dumb, cunning wit.

Their duty tries to cage him, but they see
Their own youth caged in him, and wish him free.

YOUNG MAN IN THE COUNTY JAIL

When he was small, they threatened him with prison
And living in a cell on a crust of bread.
Now he is grown, the greatest threat seems leaving
This compact safety for the bleak outside.

The jailer could be worse; food's not all that bad;
There's not much view, but outdoors there's ice and snow.
He's used to the glum furniture, the cozy mottoes.
If he has to leave, where has he got to go?

Outside, he's sure, something will happen again;
Jobs will be hard to find, the boss a driver.
He'll need money. It'll be like it was before.
He might as well do it soon so it'll be over.

He's like us all, who love our prisons more
Than life and the sad privilege to endure.

JAMIE

When Jamie was sixteen,
Suddenly he was deaf. There were no songs,
No voices any more. He walked about stunned by the terrible
    silence.
Kicking a stick, rapping his knuckles on doors,
He felt a spell of silence all about him,
So loud it made a whirring in his ears.
People moved mouths without a sound escaping:
He shuddered at the straining of their throats.
And suddenly he watched them with suspicion,
Wondering if they were talking of his faults,
Were pitying him or seeing him with scorn.
He dived into their eyes and dragged up sneers,
And sauntering the streets, imagined laughter behind him.

Working at odd jobs, ploughing, picking potatoes,
Chopping trees in the lumber woods in winter,
He became accustomed to an aimless and lonely labour.
He was solitary and unloquacious as a stone,
And silence grew over him like moss on an old stump.
But sometimes, going to town,
He was sore with the hunger for company among the people,
And, getting drunk, would shout at them for friendship,
Laughing aloud in the streets.
He returned to the woods,
And dreaming at night of a shining cowboy heaven
Where guns crashed through his deafness, woke morose,
And chopped the necks of pine trees in his anger.

THE OCTOPUS

Though she had red-gold hair, and a soft skin,
And a kind heart, and a walk with a special grace,
And a man might rest his face down on her breast
And feel secure of gentle thoughts within;

Though he loved her, and knew she loved him too,
He dreamed of an octopus that wrapped him round
With a thousand arms; or he was gagged and bound,
Unable to move, and she'd become his foe.

So bitterly he wrote her a bitter letter,
And awaited an answer from her that never came;
Was relieved and disappointed; thought it better
To have broken off cleanly; felt a little shame,
Yet told himself, to dull the ache of loss,
It's well to possess, but not to be possessed.

69

DEATH BY DROWNING

Plunging downward through the slimy water
He discovered, as the fear grew worse,
That life, not death, was what he had been after:
Ironic to die in life's symbol and source.

Drowning was not so easy as it looked from shore.
He had thought of sinking down through layers of peace
To depths where mermaids sang. He would be lapped over
By murmuring waves that lulled him into rest.

But all death is a kind of strangulation,
He had been told once and remembered now,
Choking on water like a rope, and coughing
Its bloody taste from his mouth. He had not known
Before how the body struggled to survive
And must be forced, and forced again, to die.

PROFESSOR BLAKE

Twenty years he was editor of the University Review,
Moving a comma here or a colon there,
Changing "while" to "whilst" and "except" to "save,"
Writing lengthy letters of rejection or acceptance.
An old man, pedantic in thought and dress,
Author of elegies on dogs or sonnets on Beauty,
He avoided the irregular in verse and the flamboyant in
    neckties.
His first pride was his collection of autographs,
His second that he had known John Masefield.
And he remembered having tea with Thomas Hardy,
Whose wife he thought was vulgar. But did any cold wind
From Egdon Heath blow over the jam and crumpets
And ruffle the pale brown tea in the teacups?

"You should read books on prosody," he said.
"You should try a villanelle.
You are young and impatient, and believe in love and pain
And violence and despair. You will not always believe in them.
Art is discipline and elegance. Life is not violent."

Strange that he died a violent, an absurd death,
Scalded to death in his shower. What elegy
Could turn red scalded skin to marble
Or make cold music out of that steaming corpse?

CANON BRADLEY

The Canon, pastor of a peaceful flock,
Was always all his people could desire.
Prosily pious, placidly devout,
Not given much to spend his time in prayer,
Taking his faith on faith and without doubt,
Fond of his food, his dogs, his pipe, his jokes,
Perhaps a little less fond of his wife,
Charitable and in the main good-natured.
His sermons never kept a soul awake,
But there was never any nonsense about them.
Companionable and hearty with the men,
He complimented their wives with discreet bluntness.
His round, red, cheerful face, enwreathed in smiles,
Beamed frankly out on every social meeting.

It was a pity, so the people said,
His wife was not more like him. The parson's wife
Should be more sociable, a better mixer.
But she was shy, perhaps a little cold.
She never joined the Guild or sang in the choir,
Was never active in good works, had been known to smile,
Perhaps maliciously, at those who were.
Prim and a trifle bookish, she kept aloof
From all her neighbours, from her husband too.

Their only child, their little daughter Anne,
Died suddenly when she was twelve years old,
And each endured a solitary grief.
The mother, folding up her daughter's dresses,
Bought a new lap-dog, walked the length of town,
Smiling her calm smile at the passing neighbours.
The Canon, with his round, bewildered face
No longer red, stood in his pulpit, gazed
Uncertainly about him, read his text,
Stopped in the middle of a sentence, stared
A full five minutes out the open door,
And said, "Beloved, let us meditate
On the Communion of Saints. I have nothing to say."

73

LORD MONOMARK

"Write a funny poem about Lord Monomark,"
Someone said;
And (aside from the fact that everything's been said before
And some of it very funnily indeed)
One might manage
To be amusing
About the dictatorial dinners,
The grandiose gestures,
The faddish diets
For the sake of his constipation,
Or his (gratified) desire
To see his statue put up
Before he died.

But has the age
Whose ideals he so well personified
The right to laugh
At this poor boy from a bleak background,
Scrubbed and decently semi-starved,
Reaching out for riches
To fling like blazing fireworks,
A streak-lightning of diamonds
Against the darkness?
Did he not win power
(For a time,
Of a sort)
And walk with kings,
Finding their company perhaps
Duller than his own?

But power departed,
Like youth, strength, and fame,
And only money lasted
To buy what he needed.
With his benefactions he cried,
"Love me, damn you,
Or you will be sorry."

Why should I write a funny poem
About my brother?

LEMUEL MURRAY: CONTEMPLATIVE

"The way to God in our time
is through the market place."
Nor do I deny the truth or the partial truth;
But yet I pay tribute to
Lemuel Murray, my father's friend,
Old bachelor in stubbly beard and sweaty shirt,
Who in the days when bombs were falling
Sat in his kitchen with its piles of greasy dishes
And read history at the kitchen table,
Leaning his arms on the oilcloth cover,
Stubbing his cigarettes in saucers,
Spilling ashes on the worn linoleum,
While he watched in his mind the long procession,
Alexander, Caesar, Constantine, Charlemagne,
Listened to the voices of Demosthenes or Burke.

He did not wish to use history,
To teach it, to persuade with it, to moralize on it,
To win academic honours with it
Or to get his living by it,
But only to watch the procession, the long procession
Leading to Belsen and Hiroshima.

TWO LUNACIES

My neighbour tells me
About an undertaker
In her home town, who,
Worried about his failure in business,
Stretched himself out in a coffin
And took rat poison.

But I like better
(Because anyway he was on the side of life)
That priest who caused his superiors concern
When he went wandering about Chicago
Trying to consecrate
All the bread trucks in the city.
How he must have enjoyed thinking
Of all that holy
Everyday
Bread!

ATLAS

Somebody told me about two men
Who were taking LSD—and maybe were a little drunk—
Who spent most of a night
Thinking they were supporting a bridge across the river.
It was a great responsibility,
A great strain on the muscles,
And think of all those cars
And all the pedestrians
Who might have fallen to death
If the men had dropped the bridge.

I laughed, but next day
Stayed home from work
And rested my back from supporting
My share of the world.

Lillooet

LILLOOET: A CANADIAN VILLAGE
To D.B.G. and to D.M.F.

A POEM you have asked—a long one, too.
No trifling, tiny lyric verse will do;
No sonnet to an eyebrow or a whiffletree,
No elegy to an enemy dying of sniffles he
Acquired from the cold glance of an icy eye—
In short, no small potatoes poetry,
But something grand, impressive and sublime
And guaranteed to use up years of time
In writing, if not reading. It must rhyme,
But not in stanzas ballad or Spenserian.
If theological, it should be Presbyterian
Because Catholicism is too stylish,
And at a Baptist who would bat an eyelash?

But what the subject I must write upon?
The history of the stolen Stone of Scone?
The lives and manners of the U.E. Loyalists
Explaining why they persisted in being royalists?
Cowper at least had Lady Hesketh's sofa,
But I can never manage, I fear, to shove a
Full-grown Chesterfield into my verse,
Though since you set no Task I might do worse.
Well, should I write of General MacArthur,
Communist spy trials or the laws of barter,
The Massey Commission or the Marshall Plan?
Or should I justify God's ways to man?

No, that's been done before—a task less common
Might be to justify man's ways to women,
Or woman's ways to man. But that brings sex in,
And Freud to me is dull as an election.

Election! Should I write as a Young Liberal
Or speak of Vested Interests drinking their slippersful
At popular expense? Or avoid strife
By merely praising the Canadian Way of Life?

A literary subject, now, might do—
An Essay on Criticism, or perhaps a new
Statement of what a poem ought to be
(Besides globed fruit), and where to find the key
To writing one. (There is no inspiration,
You say: but what, I ask, of exhalation?)
Should one sip tea and lie back on one's pillow,
The absorbent mind waiting for heaven to spill a
Full flood of poetry upon its blotter?
Or should one rather make it be one's motto
To sit, as I do now, biting my nails
And making faces when the subject fails,
Damning all rhymes that fly with unsalted tails?

No, none of these are good enough. My mind,
Stunted in early youth, can never find
It possible to make objective analysis,
But remains in a sort of emotional paralysis,
Unable to proceed beyond the personal.

I must write of a person, but what person will
Do to write of? It might conceivably do
To write about that wonderful person, You,
Except that, from some freak of oddity,
I prefer that still more wonderful person, Me.

I'll compromise, and write about the town
Where we were born. Not Lillooet alone
You'll see here, but you may find something out
About your Bathurst and your Sioux Lookout.

LILLOOET: A CANADIAN VILLAGE

Lillooet is the town where you were born,
Or else your child will see it in his turn.
Two sawmills and three churches, an Orange Lodge,
The school, the movie house, and a hodge-podge
Of shacks and showier houses—these make up
The village life. No visitor would stop
To take a snapshot of its streets, for they,
Without being urban, lack rusticity.
One Main Street stretches through the length of town,
From Lillooet Hotel to the fields down
By Johnny Weber's farm. A sidewalk runs
Along it, made of concrete, except once
When it becomes wood for a stretch, and boys
Coming upon it like its hollow noise.

The two big stores are Elliott's and Hill's,
Kept by the owners of the rival mills.
Here the mill workers run accounts, and learn
Their money's spent before their wage is earned.
These merchants sell both groceries and gowns,
Hammocks and hams, and sugar, spice, and spoons.

There is a Woolworth's, built not long ago,
To all the countryside a place of show,
For in it can be bought—what is thought most on—
The same things sold in Fredericton or Boston:
Shoe bags and tablecloths and dolls of plastic,
Nylon pyjamas, medicines for gastric
Complaints, photos of movie stars,
Pitchers in shape of Donald Ducks or bears,
Cheap reproductions of the Angelus,
Cushions inscribed to Mother, with a verse
Telling her virtues; cards for convalescents,
And perfumes guaranteed to raise men's passions.

More perfumes can be bought, and salves and vitamins
In the town drug store, run by Hazen Brightmans.
A Seventh Day Adventist, Hazen rests on Saturday:
His Presbyterian wife keeps shop on that day.

The drug store sells the only print in Lillooet:
The latest Pocket Books, and the shrill wit
Of *The New Yorker* for the Misses Hill;
Stories of Horror—"Every page a thrill";
Life, Time, The Saint John papers, *True Romances,*
Some movie magazines, the breathless chances
Of *Ranch Life;* and the "funnies" for the youngsters,
With their amusing tales of gangs and gunsters.

Next to the drug store is the town beautician's,
Run by Miss Betty Lou (Susannah Higgins).
Trained in Saint John, though born here, Susy has
A first-hand knowledge of all the city ways.
Sophistication marks each new coiffure
She gives her customers, and the allure
Of Hollywood is shown in manicure.
She makes each school girl think that she'd be able
(With better legs) to pass for Betty Grable.
Here, in the steamy atmosphere of Susy's
The housewife learns what all the latest news is.
Relaxed beneath the humming of the drier,
She listens to Susannah's voice go higher
In shrill excitement or sink to confidence
Telling how Prue was drunk at the last dance;
And, lulled to indiscretion, adds her bit
Of information—it must be a secret.

There is no restaurant in town but Pete's.
He serves his hamburgers and banana splits
With a shrewd jollity. His only waitress,
His daughter Dolly, a fat girl in a white dress
That makes her look like a round, snowy mountain,
Smiles moistly from behind the soda fountain,
Or wisecracks with the boys, or coyly woos them
With the loose folds of her gelatinous bosom.
The juke box sobs untruly, "I won't sigh,"
And only waits another song to die,
Perpetual chorus to that god of love
Who, with the aid of cash, makes the world move.

82

Much of Pete's business comes on movie nights—
Wednesdays and Saturdays, at Elmer Kite's.
The Capitol was built two years ago.
Before that time they used to hold the show
In the Orange Lodge, but Catholics objected,
And finally this building was erected,
Spacious and glossy, with a glittering sign,
And like the city ones in its design.

Near by, though set a little off the street,
Is the Baptist Church. There, when the people meet,
They hear the Reverend Adolphus Simples,
A pale young man, much troubled by his pimples.
When he came first to town, fresh from his college,
Adolphus wanted to display his knowledge,
To reconcile theology and science,
To quell the sceptic's ignorant defiance
By sounder reasoning, so that, over-awed,
He'd glorify Adolphus and his God.

But none were sceptics here, Adolphus found,
Unless for reasons that were most unsound
And quite unscientific. Worst of all,
They seemed to think he was heretical,
Hinted he'd have to hear another Call
If he continued to cast doubt upon
The time it took for the Creation.
So now Adolphus, to avoid offence,
Preaches the Mysteries of Providence.

83

Still he desires to be thought erudite,
And ornaments his sermons with the trite
Flowers of poetry; or, should he speak
Of the Word of God, adds, "Logos in the Greek."
His congregations feel that he adorns
His pulpit, though he cannot stop their yawns:
They proudly say, awakened from their sleep,
"The Reverend Simples' sermons sure are deep."

Adolphus is a meek and gentle man;
He gives rebukes as softly as he can.
Heaven's a reality—he knows that well,
But cannot make his mind up about Hell.
His predecessors were not always so.
Fifty or even thirty years ago
When Abner Beagle or John Holland preached
Hell was a neighbouring country, quickly reached.
They spoke of brimstone and the undying worm,
Of gnashing teeth, of hail and fiery storm,
Until their congregations shook with fear,
Expecting the Last Judgment to appear.
But now the devil and all the gnashing molars
Belong to no one but the Holy Rollers.

84

The leading members of Adolphus' flock
Are the Hill family. Built upon a rock
Their fortune never was, but rather stood
Uplifted on a pile of Lillooet wood.
Pete, the first Hill the village ever knew,
Built the first sawmill and sent out his crew
Of lumberjacks to chop the winter woods,
And, prospering, amassed much worldly goods.
A lumberjack himself from the Miramichi,
He knew both logs and men, and so could see
When nature or his crew might overreach him,
And in advance he was prepared to teach them
Respect for his superior skill and cunning.
Reaching his middle years, he thought of running
For the local legislature; of course, succeeded,
Then, feeling that a man like him was needed
In larger spheres, got himself nominated
To run for the Dominion House. He won
And thought he'd be the Premier when he'd done.

A self-made man, Pete was, of course, a Grit,
Strong for the Common Man, ready to meet
And fight on his behalf the despot Tory,
And those who fought against him would be sorry.

If he would not exactly skin alive
A villager who voted Conservative,
He might not see his way quite clear to hire him
For work next winter. Even earlier he might fire him.
All men should have a vote, so he conceded,
But, then, he thought, all men should vote as he did.

Being a Member, Pete could settle down
To rule his church, his family, and his town.
No Baptist clergyman would dare to preach
A doctrine other than King Pete would teach.
Five strapping sons and three tall daughters trembled
To hear his voice, when they were all assembled
For evening and for morning prayers and scoldings.
No villager, except some stubborn old ones,
Or farmers on the outskirts—always bold ones—
Would dream of voting other than Liberal
All were subordinate to Pete's strong will.

Truly enough, indeed, within the House
He represented his constituents' views
And told the assembled spokesmen of the nation
His people, diddled at Confederation
And burdened by Canadian taxation
Ought to secede if, in their humble view,
The Maritimes did not receive their due.
Why this expensive railway to the West?
Could not the country ever seem to rest
Content with what it had? The member opposite
(A man he'd grant had eloquence and wit)
Spoke pridefully of an illimitable nation.
Illimitable, indeed, was the taxation.
Why this eternal worry about size?
What value had a big and worthless prize?
After the limitless West, must we go forth
To sow the barren acres of the North,
While still New Brunswick lay wrapped in her woods
Unpillaged of the riches of her goods?
This growth that sapped an undeveloped land
Was not a healthy growth and could not stand.
Huge, but not great, the country would become,
A sprawling monster waiting for its doom.

86

Few men in Lillooet would not have agreed
With Pete Hill's words; though, rather than secede,
Some of the younger men were glad to go
Out West, or even to Ontario.

More sought their fortunes crossing into Maine:
New England sent their fathers, and again
Received the sons and grandsons to her bosom,
This time with little fear that she would lose them.
But many stayed, for Lillooet still stands,
Though worms have eaten Pete's broad, folded hands
Since thirty years ago he first was laid
In the Lillooet graveyard's heavy-hanging shade,
A man of ninety taking his first rest
Beneath his favourite spruce, facing the east.

Twenty years in the Commons he had sat
And thirty in the Senate after that;
But in the last ten years he rarely spoke.
There was about him at that time a look
As of one listening for a once-known voice,
Whether it was a friend's or enemy's.
Here with these younger men who did not know
The hopes and quarrels of times long ago,
He sat and, nodding in the quiet room,
He heard far-off their voices' muted hum
Fade to the roaring of the Miramichi
Running through distant woods to meet the sea.
Long since he'd found that Grits no more than Tories
Cared for New Brunswick Rights or such old stories.
Canada's Century, not New Brunswick's, this:
New Brunswick and not Canada was his.
But what was time? It was in his command.
He held his childhood waiting in his hand.
And so he turned from thoughts of present wrong
To days when he and Lillooet were young.

In his old age he built the house that still
Belongs to his first grandson, Richard Hill,
A great white wooden structure, finished well,
Almost as big as the Lillooet Hotel.

Here, with his rooms beneath his gloating gaze
He told his guests how, in his younger days,
He used the top of a barrel for a table,
Built his first bed with boards, and would be able
To knock a chair together still, if need be,
Though not one fine enough to please a lady.
He filled the house with love seats and long mirrors,
Toy china dogs, and vine-encircled chairs,
And twenty clocks, to tell the time to one
Whose only time-piece once had been the sun.
But since Pete's death his furniture has vanished,
By auction sold or to the attic banished,
Except such things as Mrs. Richard can
Call true Antiques, and fit into her plan.
Most people think the place improved a lot,
For Mrs. Dick has Taste and Pete had not.

Her living room might come from *Homes and Gardens*,
And any villagers who are allured once
Into its softly lit and carpeted shade
Are envious, pleased, admiring and dismayed
To see a room that's twice as big again
As all their downstairs. Such a job to clean!
The fireplace, with the coffee table near
On which a book may now and then appear
Elaborately open, as though to prove
That Mrs. Richard has a genuine love
For true good reading; the carpet in pale blue
With matching draperies at the windows, through
Which the visitor may obtain a view
Of a green lawn where beds of flowers are laid
Under the maple's patriotic shade—
These are the proofs that Mrs. Dick has given
That she is capable of Gracious Living.

Her quiet library is a pleasant place.
The bulky Hansards—grave and portly race—
Prove that the father and grandfather still
Are honoured by the family of Hill;
And Pete's fierce portrait glares across the room
As though he spoke Confederation's doom.

A slightly smaller picture of Dick's father,
James Hill, M.P., stares at him from the other
Side wall. Most of the books are his.
"Clever, but queer," the village said he was.
He died before King Pete, and therefore none
Could know how well he would have ruled alone.

"Solid, of course, but hardly fresh today,"
Mrs. Dick, looking at the books will say.
"And even in his time he did not choose
Awfully well: he never read reviews."

The Book-of-the-Month Club once supplied her books,
But, since her daughters scorn this, now she looks
At the Saturday Review of Literature,
And so can feel that she's superior
In brains as in position to Mrs. Simples
And the young doctor's wife, a girl whose dimples
And pleasant, blank expression make her agreeable
As a frequent guest at the afternoon tea-table.

She's fond of sketching—does it rather well
And the Baptist Church and the Lillooet Hotel
Are often shown to her admiring guests;
She points out how the church's shadow rests
Along the grass (shadows are hard to do),
And sighs, and says it's really sad how few
Appreciate how difficult Art is,
And it's in this and Music that her heart is.
The world, she thinks, would no more be at strife
If people loved the Finer Things of Life.
Her dining room at night is candle-lit.
Vulgar electric—she'd not think of it;
And Mr. Simples, peering through the gloom,
Praises his hostess for her tasteful room.
Indeed, the food's so good, he compliments
Her beauty, wit, charm and intelligence.

Young Dr. Mack lives just across the street,
In the same house where once his father kept
His shingle out—old Dr. Mack, whose name
Still has in Lillooet its local fame.
The Country Doctor! Legendary man
Who once could do what now no mortal can,
With his one horse cross mountainous drifts of snow
On country roads where no one else would go;
Tireless, good-humoured, endlessly charitable,
Lengthening his treatment, shortening his bill.

Such is the legend, but in fact the truth is
That old Doc Mack was in his time a ruthless
Collector of accounts—would collect twice
If a receipt was lost. His lowest price
Was the highest he could ask, and if complained to—
There were doctors in Saint John if they'd a mind to
Go that far off, he said. He did not object
To the winter roads—that's true enough, and yet
He often was too drunk even to come
To a patient a few houses from his home.
Still, people either died or they got well:
Whichever happened, Doc could send his bill.
Midwives were handy, women healthy then,
And one child dead still left another ten.

On a small side street branching off from Main
The village school stands. You can see it plain
Some distance off, for it has room inside
To hold the kids from all the countryside
For miles around. They come from Higgins Mills,
Gaspereaux Flat, Wekusko, and Blue Hills
And half-a-dozen nameless communities,
Prepared to struggle for the dubious prize
Of education, which their parents imagine
Will enable them to bring a better wage in.

When June has come, and with it graduation,
The assembled parents meet in congregation
To see their children winning their diplomas,
And even the grandpas and the grandmamas
Look on with pride. Anne Brightmans plays the piano
(She's in Grade Ten. Her relatives think Anne a
Regular genius) while the twelfth-grade girls
Come trooping down the aisle, elaborate curls
Framing their anxious faces, the white swirls
Of their long dresses sweeping along the ground
As, solemn-faced, not daring to look around
The buzzing room, they mount the platform where
They spend the evening, suffering the stare
Of the assembled village. After them the boys
Clump to the platform, drowning with their noise
Their families' whispers. Then "O Canada"
Is sung, and the principal rises to command a
Silence for the speaker of the occasion,
A man he's sure is well known to the nation,
The Provincial Minister of Education.
Mr. McQueen has kindly given consent
To speak to them; indeed a compliment
To the citizens of Lillooet! To introduce
Him is unnecessary, but they will excuse
A few words summarizing Mr. M.'s career
And telling how he happens to be here.

Mr. McQueen is happy to be able
To address the class, though not as capable
As many others present, he is certain.
These fresh young faces almost disconcert him
So idealistically looking to the future.
And that is right, for they should really note here
That they've begun, not ended, education.
New things to learn, new problems will be facing
Them in the days to come, but he is sure
They'll meet them with that courage to endure
And dare and do that always characterizes
Canadian youth, and brought the victories
Their elder brothers won in the last war.

These post-war days have problems too, and more
Than ever previously they must beware
Of groups that cause disharmony and strife
And undermine the Canadian Way of Life.
Three things they must not ever fail to prize:
Democracy, the Crown, Free Enterprise.

Young Mr. Maybee is the next to speak,
The Anglican clergyman. During all the week
He's practised this speech and next Sunday's sermon,
But now he cannot manage even to worm one
Extra sentiment from his mind, not said
Already by Mr. McQueen. He wishes him dead
For having stolen what he wanted to say,
But adds that they must take the time to pray
To the Heavenly Father in these times of stress,
And lead a life of upright humbleness.

93

"John Peel" is sung by half the high school boys,
And then the girls in chorus give advice
To go in lilac time to visit Kew—
Something few present much intend to do.
Then come the Class Will and Class Prophecy:
In fifteen years Rose Anna is to be
A movie star, Bill Tompkins a prize fighter;
Hugo will patent a new cigarette lighter;
Roy Donaldson will sit in Parliament,
Although evicted for not paying rent;
A Roller preacher, much oppressed by sins,
Jim Hays will have ten children and two chins.

Last comes the Valedictory, and farewell
Is said by Sue Hawkes on behalf of all
Her fellow classmates: A farewell to teachers,
Parents and friends and school trustees and preachers,
To town's people—they all have been most kind—
Whose image they will cherish in their minds.

A most affecting speech, the parents say,
And fondly pause to wipe a tear away,
Until this recollection drives away their sorrow—
They're sure to see them all again tomorrow.

To the left of the school house is the Post Office.
No family in town would ever miss
A daily visit to the wicket, where
Miss Aggie Cozens hands to each his share
Of letters. When Miss Aggie was still young
She read romantic novels over-long.

Then earls and countesses in coronets,
Governesses married to young baronets,
Ladies who swept their mantle's silken train
Through mirrored corridors with high disdain—
These made a small commotion in her brain
That blew away her little share of sense.
She was persuaded that some lucky chance
Would bring to Lillooet a British Peer:
When his eyes lighted on her, she'd appear
More lovely than cold-hearted Lady Blanche
Who'd jilted him last year, and soon they'd launch
On some grand ship to cross the fierce Atlantic.
His haughty mother would at first be frantic
To hear he'd married a Canadian bride,
But when she saw her she could scarcely chide
A girl with manners so genteel and sweet,
Though wishing that he'd made a more discreet
Match in a social sense. And when a year
Had passed, and the first baby could appear,
She'd melt, just looking at the little dear,
And say, "For Baby's Sake you are forgiven:
Your marriage certainly was made in Heaven."

This dream made Aggie in her time refuse
To go with any Lillooet man. She'd choose
No lumberjack or mill-hand—no, nor farmer,
Butcher or druggist, though that was getting warmer.

A teacher, though he might have some gentility,
Yet was most certainly lacking in the ability
To supply luxuries. A lawyer might have done,
Or doctor, but in Lillooet there were none
Except old Mack, who was already married,
And so poor Aggie's little plans miscarried.

No baron ever visited Lillooet,
But in her Office Aggie's waiting yet.
Her manner has a certain air of state,
As of a woman expecting to be great,
And when she speaks, her high-flown sentences
Issue with what she thinks a languid grace.
Yet those who pity her, or idly laugh,
Are scarcely justified in sigh or scoff.
To call her foolish would be to misjudge her.
Would she be happier married to the butcher?

East of the village is Tarpaper Town,
The slum of Lillooet, with its tumbledown
Tarpaper shanties, only slightly more
Luxurious than the backhouse at each door.
Some of the houses have one room, some two—
A kitchen-dining room and a room that'll do
As bedroom for five children and their parents.
Sometimes two families in a house share rents
And so can manage something much more grand.
Behind each shack is a small plot of land
Where ragged rows of weeds and vegetables
Grow for the gracing of the family tables.
Tarpaper Town houses the bootleggers,
The drunks, the down-and-out who, not quite beggars
But nearly so, live more on hope than money;
Some young couples living on bread and honey
And quantities of love; and one or two
Families that are more prosperous, but who
Find it cheaper to build their houses there
Than in the rest of Lillooet; they care
More for appearances than do their neighbours,
And, looking at the fruits of evening labours,
Their neatly-painted houses, are angry that
Tarpaper Town's not called East Lillooet.

Among the houses of a neater sort
Is that where Ruby Mullins lived. Report
Had it that two of Ruby's sons
Belonged to Pete Hill's second boy, and once
The Presbyterian preacher was her flame.
Doc Mack, though much her elder, had his name
Connected with hers. All her children were
Handsome or clever, though both dark and fair,
Blue-eyed and brown-eyed, frail and muscular.
Ruby herself, even in her younger days,
Was not a beauty, though her ruddy face
With its wholesome country freshness was a pleasure
To look at; and though good enough, the measure
Of hips and bust did not show true proportion.
Rawboned and lanky, she must move with caution,
Or else the furniture she touched came crashing.
Her eyes protruded, though the green lights flashing
Within their depths gave her a look of fun.
She wore her thick, bleached hair in a round bun
At the nape of her neck. She had no touch of style,
And yet she won you with her ready smile.
She greatly disapproved of prostitution
As being hard on any constitution,
And only slept with men because they were
People she liked and very fond of her.

97

As she grew older she became devout.
At the Roller Tabernacle the hoarse shout
Of Ruby's voice was often heard in song,
Or in the Testimonials, with their long
Accounts of sins forgiven and trials past,
Judgment escaped, Salvation won at last.
She much admired one of the Roller preachers,
A grave young man with most angelic features,
And when she died ("passed peacefully away,"
The Saint John paper said) one April day,
He preached a sermon on her beauteous spirit
That would have made even Ruby cry to hear it.

One of the leading Roller members was
Sam Perry. In the past his violent ways,
His drinking and his swearing made his wife
Tell all the neighbours he led her a life
She'd never wish on any other woman.
Sam had a face that scarcely proved him human,
His features were so near-Neanderthal.
Some jokers said no other proof at all
Was needed to uphold the Darwinian theory
Except Sam's face, especially when, beery
After a visit to a neighbouring bootlegger's,
He wandered home in a great fit of staggers.
He scarcely had a forehead, and his nose
Must have been flattened by some heavy blows.
His eyes were beady under shaggy brows.
His chest and arms were covered with black hair
So thick another beast would call it fur.
Though short and squat, he had uncommon strength
And bullied many men of greater length,
For he loved fighting even more than whisky
And people feared him nights when he grew frisky.

When Sam was made a convert, his behaviour
Became more pleasing to his Heavenly Saviour.
He never drank, he rarely beat his wife,
And promised to give swearing up for life.
When angered, to avoid some stronger word,
He yelled out "Hallelujah! Praise the Lord!"
And all his neighbours were compelled to own
Sam was a model for Tarpaper Town.

But miracles are rarely everlasting,
And even saints grow tired of prayers and fasting.
Poor Sam grew weary of his penitence
And sought about for causes of offence.
One Sunday a new preacher came to town,
A powerful speaker, who sent all those down
To Hell he disapproved of. With a groan
Of anguished pleasure, he recounted to them
The torrid tortures that he thought were due them.

"There in the flames," he cried, "will be your mothers,
Who idolized strange gods; your elder brothers,
Who scorn you now, will cry to you for water,
As though to Lazarus, to ease their lot there.
And you, reposing then in Abraham's bosom,
Will find it your sad duty to refuse them."

Sam, who'd been sitting dozing in his seat,
Rose and called out, "Friends, this is where I quit.
I'll go and see my family in Hell.
They and my friends are likely keeping well.
And, as for water, if the pumps all fail,
We'll still have whisky and a little ale."

When winter comes, most of the men and boys
Leave Lillooet for the woods. Elliott employs
The larger number, but the Hills still have
Several crews in the woods. Both companies leave
The management of crews to the little bosses,
The petty Main Johns, who, with men and horses,
Bring the logs to the river, where they wait
Until the ice is thawed by the Spring heat
And the Drive begins. But Spring is far away
When the men are first in camp. The working day
Is long. They're up before the dawn
And eat their pork and pancakes while the sun
Is gathering its strength. The frosty air
Makes the sharp sound of axe-blades carry clear,
And warning rustle of the toppling trees,
Breaking the hush of winter silences.

In the evenings, when they've made their meal-time jokes
About sour biscuits and still sourer cooks,
Or soggy doughgods, underdone potatoes,
And pies not fit to give the starving dagoes,
They turn to talk of camps where they have been
In other winters. Some of them have seen
Camps in Quebec or in the State of Maine.
Some have been Out West all the way to Vancouver,
And wonder why they ever came to move here.

Cookhouses there, they say, have radios;
The camps have shower baths; not a single louse
Escapes alive. In fact, the place would suit
The members of a Women's Institute.

Sometimes a man will get his fiddle out;
He'll choose the song, the rest in chorus shout,
Perhaps a song heard on the radio,
Or a come-all-ye the old-timers know,
"Peter Emberley" or "Banks of Gaspereaux";
Sometimes the camp's own song-maker will tell
In rugged rhyme of how the spruce logs fell
When Jim and Paul contested with each other;
Then some old-timer minds how well his father
Could make up songs. "There was a man you'd praise.
He'd rhyme till he was black and blue in the face.
Give him a subject—anything you'd want
Senator Hill, your mother's maiden aunt,
The cook's baked beans, the beauty of a broom—
He'd spiel off verses till the cows came home,
And never stop to think or catch his breath.
There's been nobody like him since his death."

In Spring logs fill Trout River near the town,
And ice and logs together, drifting down,
Make the river seem a solid, sluggish mass
Until it comes to the sawmills. When you pass
These mills, you hear their daily throb and scream,
A sound as though they were alive. They seem
To own the village and its men and goods,
Rivers and fields and tributary woods.

At the Lillooet Hotel, where Main Street ends,
Bridge Road begins, and at right angles extends,
Crossing the river, site of both the mills,
And curving upward through the neighbouring hills
Past ragged farm yards, bosomed deep in weeds,
Where slumber cows as withered as their feeds;

Past lonely mail-boxes, where women stand
With waiting eyes; past woods on either hand,
Gray birches like a million ghosts in line,
Or the red branches of a blighted pine,
The heavy grace of stands of fir and spruce
Casting the sullen shadow of their boughs
Upon the passer-by (from such trees' wood
The people of Lillooet earn their daily food);
Past other Lillooets under other skies,
Past cities swallowing Lillooet in size;
Past plains and mountains to another ocean
Tossing its many heads in wild commotion.
Sweet Lillooet! Grimiest village of the plain,
I may not see your Baptist church again,
Or in old age find refuge here at last
To meditate upon the blissful past;
But I am sure I'll find your population
In any town or city in the nation.
No matter where I live, my neighbour still
Will be Miss Ruby Mullins or Pete Hill.

Narratives

THE TWO HELENS

Helen, the story goes,
Was never in Troy town:
The gods made an image
And wrapped it in her gown,

And with this false lady
Lustful Paris lay,
Not with the real Helen—
So the stories say.

Helen, true Helen
Was carried swift and far
To a lonely island
Where she knelt in prayer,

Prayed for Menelaus
Every day and night
While the false Helen
Swam in soft delight.

While the false Helen
Tasted Paris' mouth,
True Helen wasted
Away her bitter youth.

While the false Helen
Slept in Paris' bed,
True Helen laid on stone
Her lonely head.

103

False, fatal Helen,
Which was really you,
The beautiful false image
Or the true?

MRS. PERDITA ROBINSON AND
THE PRINCE OF WALES

She acted in The Winter's Tale
The night the Prince came.
Before the curtains rose
There was talk in the green-room.

The witty Mr. Smith
Said, to her delight,
"By Jove, Mrs. R.,
You'll win the Prince tonight."

She stood before the royal box
And curtsied to her judge.
In the royal presence
She blushed beneath her rouge.

A stately fairy prince,
Inclined to corpulence,
He looked, he leered, he loved:
She had no defence.

Such beauty in a man
She never saw till now:
A sceptre in his gaze,
An empire in his brow.

His eyes lay on her eyes
Like fingers on her breast.
Condescendingly,
He nodded to her twice.

He wrote her a letter
That was uncommon civil.
She was his shepherd maid,
He was her Florizel.

He sent her his picture
With a paper heart,
Saying that to Perdita
He'd be faithful to death.

They met in Kew gardens
When the moon shone still.
Their midnight conversations
Were always rational.

He wrote her another letter,
Said, "We must meet no more."
She tried to see him,
But was turned from the door.

Walking at Hyde Park Corner,
She saw him pass.
He turned away his head
To avoid her face.

She wrote a mournful poem,
Then dried her tears.
With the brave Colonel Tarleton
She lived sixteen years.

A NARRATIVE OF A SINGULAR IMPOSITION

She appeared at a cottage door
Wearing a turban
And speaking a language
Known to no man.

They took her to Mr. Worrall
And his lady,
Who knew as many languages
As anybody;

But they made nothing of her,
Only that her name
Was Caraboo. A princess
They thought she seemed.

Her features were fine,
Her complexion brown,
Her disposition gentle,
Her eyes cast down.

Her mode of diet seemed
To be Hindoostanic;
She ate no meat
And no beer drank.

She said her prayers
On top of the roof,
Fasted every Tuesday
Of her life.

They tried to find her language
With the Polyglot Bible
And Fry's Pantographia,
But they were not able.

But she picked up English
After a while,
And told them pirates brought her
From her native soil.

At home she wore a headdress
Of seven peacock feathers
To show how great a chieftain
Was her father.

Some said she was Circassian,
Some said Chinese.
They had her portrait painted
In her native dress.

Lords and ladies met her;
She lived in clover
Till an old landlady saw her
And the play was over.

Poor Mary Wilcox,
Born in country hay;
Her father beat her up,
And she ran away;

Went into service
And left again;
Took shelter in a home
For fallen women,

But got put out,
Since she hadn't fallen yet;
Then had a baby
To make matters right;

Went about with gypsies,
Begged on the street,
Nearly hanged herself,
But thought better of it.

Poor Princess Caraboo—
What must have been her pain
To be Mary Wilcox
Once again?

LATE MARRIAGE

They were married at forty, having waited long
For such domestic bliss;
She had nursed the last years of her parents,
He had supported his.

Somehow, however, they were not prepared
For the boredom and intimacy
Of life together. They felt too tight
The strangulating tie.

On their honeymoon he took long walks
Looking for any strange stone.
She sat in their hotel room
With a cold in the head, alone.

On the train home she sat and grumbled
At the way he slurped his soup,
And he told her she was lucky
That he didn't drink or take dope.

When their only son was born
He was little and frail and red,
And he cried and cried all night
And kept them up from their bed;

And when he grew older they quarrelled
About what he should wear and eat,
And about his education,
And the toys he should have as a treat.

The boy grew up and disliked them
And left them alone with each other.
The father retired and grew roses
And grumbled away at the mother.

The mother spent all her time dusting,
And dusting, and dusting again,
Until she grew tired and took sick,
And the sickness addled her brain;

And she died, and her husband sat
Beside her stone still face
And wept for the youth they had never had
And the long years' waste.

PASTORAL

The park was peaceful,
The park was shady,
Where the lover walked
With his handsome lady.

Winds were soft
In their blowing hair.
The springtime flowers
Grew everywhere.

In tidy plots
The tulips stood,
Some milk pale,
Some red as blood.

Children played
By the shallow pond
And floated ships
From hand to hand;

But the lovers walked
Away from them
Through the thick green grass
As though in a dream.

Shady and peaceful
Was the place
Where they sat down
To rest for a space,

And still the spot,
Without a breath,
Where the lady stabbed her lover
To his death.

Songs and Sonnets

ONLY THE SUBTLE THINGS

Only the subtle things,
The slender, still things stand;
The heavy mountains crumble down
To fluid wastes of sand;

The medalled heroes die,
The shouting millions pass,
And on their sunken graves there grows
The mute, tenacious grass.

THE LONELINESS THAT WRAPPED HER ROUND

The loneliness that wrapped her round
Was thick as drifted snow,
So thick it seemed to make a sound
Like birds that come and go,
Like startled birds that flap their wings,
And rise, and flutter low.

So thick the air lay on her breast,
As still as vanished mirth;
"Suppose," she thought in that still night,
"Suppose this air were earth."

GRANITE'S NOT FIRM ENOUGH

Granite's not firm enough
To stay my mind;
I must in harder stone
Foundation find.

Fire cannot burn enough,
Ice cannot freeze.
Some fiercer agony
Heal my disease.

Steel cannot cut me true
To touch the bone;
Sharper blade must divide
To make me one.

EVICTION

I should have cut my life
Down to essential bone,
Paring all falsenesses:
I should have sought the sun

To burn away
The excesses of my pride;
In order to have lived
I should have died.

But, lingering in shade
And softnesses,
I rented vacancy
Thinking I purchased ease;

And would be tenant still,
Paying my life as fee,
If the sheriff pain
Had not evicted me.

114

TRUTH

To tell the truth, however much you want it,
Is a kind of hoped impossibility:
Every omission is a kind of lie,
Every admission in some way is slanted.

To hear the truth through layers of simulation
Is to be wiser than most men can bear
To be—or have their friends be, on occasion—
Though love and justice both sit in your ear.

To find the truth, you can't take the king's highway,
The straight wide road that runs from town to town.
You have to wander some circuitous byway.
The hills are like that one you travel down
And think you're going up. Walk opposite
To where truth stands, and you'll bump into it.

NO: MY LOVE WAS NOT DIVINE

No: my love was not divine.
Human or animal
It moved towards you, as the dumb
Creatures that cannot tell
Spoken caresses turn
Towards the hoped return.

To lay my head,
Safe on your arm,
So that all hovering harm
Might flee my bed

Was all I wanted, just;
As birds might rest,
Or want to, some long flight
On a strange nest.

It seemed that bodies turned
Thus each to each
Might find a plainer comfort than the mind
Could ever reach,

Wheel though it might in sublime altitude:
Is soul so wise
To pursue always to the infinite
The stubborn skies?

Is not the body wiser, tunnelling
Into the dark interior, secure,
To lay the seeds of its eternities
Where they may best endure?

FAILURE

As some poor bird that thinks
Windows are made of air
Buffets the solid glass
In its despair,

I thought what shone between us
Was film so light
A moth's wing would break it,
Or a gnat's bite.

Now on the window ledge
The dying bird
Gasps with its broken neck,
Dizzy, unheard.

117

ALL YOU WHO SIT AND WRITE

All you who sit and write
In quiet rooms apart
Letters to distant friends
Thinking you show your heart;

Or you hemmed in with crowds
Who fancy in the press
Some mind that knows your mind,
Some comprehending face:

Talk to the dead, whose hearts
Beat free from caging bone;
Talk to the rocks and winds;
Talk to the child unborn,

But not to flesh and blood,
The deaf, the obdurate ear.
The dead, the unborn may comfort you:
The living cannot hear.

I HAVE SEEN FLOWERS GROWING

I have seen flowers growing
Out of the dark sky,
Bursting their golden glowing
Hearts of infinity.

I have seen flowers shining
From banks of snow,
In white wreaths twining
Soft and slow.

I have seen green moss creeping
On stone as hard
As the lips of anger
Or a lost friend's regard.

From cold, dark, and hardness
Blossoms may rise
White as the strawberry blossoms,
Strange as the skies.

119

NIGHT FEAR

I do not know
If I really love you
Or if what I want
In your arms
Is just protection
Against the dark, against space,
The wide, lonely world
Outside.
It is as though I walked
A child
Shivering
Down a dark hall
Into my parents' bedroom
To find shelter again
In warmth of bodies
And the smell of human sweat.
I could not sleep
In my own empty room
Because it was so full
Of night.
I am frightened of the dark.
Hold me.

I THINK OF YOU

In the night I think of you
And of how my ghost might walk
Into the house where you lie sleeping,
And you would be surrounded
By people you love
Or who love you.
And in the day time I think,
You are busy, you are surrounded by people.

I am ashamed that sometimes I wish
You were alone in the world,
Poor, despised, shabby, neglected,
So that I could hold you in my arms
And comfort you
For everything you wanted,
As I wish you could comfort me
For what I want
And do not have
And long for.

POEM FOR A DRAWING BY BRUNO BOBAK

Lovers who once in caves
Or secret places
Found each a private world
In love's embraces,

Who inward turned
To mouth or breast,
Or, drowning in each other's eyes,
Sank into rest,

Must now look out again
At worlds of Arctic frost
Where wild beasts snarl for food
And paradise is lost.

THE NATURE OF THE SUBLIME

Tigers were once sublime,
Or any angry beast,
And so were lightning strokes
Or bitter smell or taste—

The taste of brine or tears,
Or stench of curdled blood,
The look of sea or plain,
Or mountain white and rude,

And kings in bright array
And armies clothed with power,
And tall and lofty winds—
All forces that devour.

Alas, the true sublime
Is sadly out of date.
To what can I compare
The power of love or hate?

Stock-piled nation high,
All human forces dwell
In an atomic passion,
Sublime, funereal.

ON CONSIDERING LILIES

Let me not try to be, or do,
Or write, or think, but all day through
Sit here by the river's side
And watch the ripples where they glide,

The birds that on the ripples play,
Or screech, like unoiled doors, all day,
The cars that on the other shore
Slide by with hint of alien power.

Let me be rooted as this tree
That is, and does not try to be,
But drops its gradual golden leaves
As softly as the water moves.

Or if, like other living things,
I shift my place, though without wings,
May I be like the birds, that move
In liquid motions of pure love,

Or butterflies with quivering touch,
Or clouds, or winds that eager rush,
Or snow, or tides, or stars, or fire,
Moved as their inward laws require.

124

ESSENTIALS

What do we need for life?
Bread, water, air,
The earth beneath our feet,
The flame of fire.

Such simplicities,
So hackneyed smooth,
Our spoiled souls scorn them plain,
Would have them clothed.

Our bread must be enriched,
Our water wine,
Our air perfumed,
Our fire confined.

But underneath the skin
Of our diseased desire
Still all our needs
Are water, earth, and fire,

And bread, and maybe love,
And, after living, death,
That with its earthen hand
Will stop our breath.

Elegies

THE EGOIST DEAD

In the cool, impersonal room
Bathed by darkness now he lies.
Silence, settling grain by grain,
Presses downward on his eyes.

Never will the untiring clock
Tick him back to prayer or lust;
Hate and benevolence lie dead,
And even the unfailing "I" is dust.

Eternity, that seemed to stretch
Elastic-like at his command,
Finds a neat and compact space
In the hollow of his hand.

SORROW, THE BIRD OF DEATH

Sorrow, the bird of death, that gnaws
Your ever-breeding Tityos-meat,
Conceals no honey in his jaws
To make your tortures sweet;

Though others, born to luckier fates,
May find felicitous relief
Proclaiming from the carven tomb
Melodious and proportioned grief;

In their inverted ecstasies
Measure the tears that beat Styx shore,
Or cry, like Poe's preposterous bird,
In neat poetics, "Nevermore."

127

PASSAGE OF SUMMER

It was a long summer, watching my father die,
A cold summer, though, with wind and rain.
    "I remember," once he told me,
"The time my father died. I was nine years old.
They couldn't tear me away, I remember.
And I remember playing in the caves
By the sea shore, gathering shells.
I remember your grandmother, after she died, came to me
In a dream and said, 'Come, Johnnie, come.'"

He woke and slept and slept and woke again,
And said "Is it day or night? Why are you going to bed
When it's noon outside? But it's such a dark day now."

"There was a joke I used to tell," he said.
"Maybe it was about Pat and Mike or maybe it was about Sandy
    and Mac,
But now I can't remember. Did I ever tell you that joke?
You would have laughed. I think it was a good one."

"This morning," he said, "I was telling your mother about you.
I thought you had never met before, and I must explain
Just who you were, but then she said she knew you."

"I wish," he said, "I could start all over again,
Have the same time over again, but different.
Only eighty years. I wish I could be young."

And then, "I am so tired, so tired, so tired.
I wish it were over."
                    Then, "Do you suppose, maybe
A cigarette, or maybe a pill for the pain?"

ELEGY FOR MY MOTHER

Dear ghost, I should have written you an elegy;
But what am I to say? What is there left
Of that child who, seventy some years ago,
Played house on a rock with a neighbour boy,
Admired her mother in strawberry coloured silk
(For Sundays only), or hid frightened in a corner
When grandmother had a tantrum? Or where now
Is the young girl demure in muslin, hair in puffs,
Who sat in the village choir and whispered and giggled
Behind the preacher's back? Or the grave face
That looked from your wedding picture with hopeful
   seriousness?

Where are you now
As my childhood saw you, with your waving hair
Pouring its midnight down your shoulders,
Or piled up, growing gray? Where is your quick step
As we went for walks together? Where (so lately)
Is the face weary with pain and the dragging step?
Where, even, that last foreign mask of you,
Dead in your coffin, which I touched with fingers
Questioning its dry coolness? You are gone away,
Your dresses empty, your get-well cards thrown out,
The sympathy notes answered, the undertaker paid.

Can finality be more final? And yet somehow
These summer afternoons with wind in the leaves
Which you would have liked to feel,
And bird song in the air, and a band playing down the street,
Is there not so much life here that somehow, somewhere
You too must share it? Are you not still here
In sunshine and the quietness of grass?

DEATHS

I remember how my mother
Before she died
Saw birds nesting
In the bottom of the bathtub.
"Cheep, cheep!" she said.
"See their bright eyes."
And she whistled at one
To make him turn his head.
I almost thought
I could see him myself.

My grandmother dressed herself
The morning she died
And walked to the outhouse, singing
"Nearer my God to thee."

My nephew skated to death
On Christmas skates.
His mother told him
To skate close to shore
And he would be safe.
He obeyed her, and drowned.

130

My teacher threw himself
From the top floor of a department store
Down to the sidewalk
And broke his neck.
The notes for next day's lecture
On T. S. Eliot
Fell from his head.

My cousin, having survived
Five years of active service
As a wartime pilot,
Smashed into a freight train
With his car and two small children.
I do not know if he was drunk or not.

And there was that man we all knew
(What was his name?)
Who died to save a child from burning.
The child died too.

OCTOBER WIND

All day the wind has blown
Through the peach-and-plum-coloured leaves of mild October
Whispering "Ripeness is all" to aster and oat stubble,
To the last of the goldenrod or to bare ground.

And if death were only this,
This sweet season
Of honey-gold cloying sun,
Bonfire and harvest home,
Then who would complain of death's kiss?

But soon the wind will blow another way.
The white fury of age
Will scream scream scream
Down the bare fields,
Ripping branches from trees,
Crashing into the dream
Of old men asleep in the dark village.

Age is a cold season,
A bare season. Who would live
Through those days of empty, blowing wind
When all that stays the mind
Is the roar of storm
Or the soft, cold drift of snow
Sifting against fences
And into the mounds of graves?

132

POEM FOR THE FEAST OF ALL SOULS

Cold the November wind;
No more the leaves
Shine on the autumn boughs;
The chill earth grieves
Covered with brown heaps
Dusty and deep as graves.

Shall I have faith
That leaves again
Rise up, the buried grain
Becomes the Corn King overcoming death?
Shall I indeed have faith?

How faint and sweet
The odour of the corpses of the leaves
Crumbling to soft decay.
But we are not as they,
And our corruption is not neat.

It is a wholesome thought,
A worthy and a gracious thing to pray
For those who died in God
And yet who stay
Waiting the triumph of their Easter day.

133

It is just and right indeed that we remember
Those lives which once were green
And shaded us from too much sun or rain;
Those lives which triumphed in a golden age
And now have gone beyond the winter's rage.
Right and just it is that we remember,

And right that we recall
Those whom we never saw but yet who gave
Words, music, life even from the grave:
Herbert and Vaughan, Crabbe, Hopkins, Blake, I call
Your names and others loved as well.

And yet how many unremembered names
That I have never known
Surround me with their love and labour past
And may be nearer grown,
More closely tied to me than those I seem
To love more in this present dream.

In dark November then
I pray for these unknown.
Unknown, pray you for me
That we may meet and never die.

134

LOCAL GRAVEYARD

In the great echoing vault of history
Our names are not heard.
Less than conquerors, we were not at Marathon,
And if we died in battle it was the mud
And not the battle we were most aware of.
More likely we died of cholera or old age
In a dark, closed room with a spoon and a medicine bottle
On a table by our beds.

The tombstone in the family plot
(With the finger pointing to the sky
Above the carved motto, "God is love")
Lists James Malachi, aged 73,
And Henrietta Charlotte, his dear wife,
Departed this life 1842, aged 39.
There are also three little children,
Aged nine, six, and three months,
Their names surmounted by the text, "Come unto Me."
No doubt, too, there are other tombstones,
Plainer or more elaborate, in many graveyards
On this continent and others.
Ours is a large family.

We were not torn by lions or burned as martyrs,
Never saw St. Paul or even John Wesley,
But were preached to by William Black of Nova Scotia,
Went to prayer meeting and confessed our sins
When we remembered them. In these dark woods
Is not loneliness terrible as a thousand lions?

Our worries were the worries of all times:
Keeping the roof above us, the children fed.
We knew the perversity of weather and crops,
Counted up the cost of clothes and tools,
Feared the advance of the great enemies,
Poverty, sickness, age, death.

Now we no longer fear them.

Sons, daughters (soon to be brothers and sisters
When death makes us all contemporary)
Do not forget us because we were not great men.
It is we, more than saints, soldiers, or poets
Who have broken the soil for you,
Built houses and languages for you,
Taught you your A B C and your recipes and prayers,
Told you the jokes you still tell at parties,
Planted the trees in your streets.

Remember us for a while, in the rustling of the leaves,
Before disease finally rots the elms,
And before you too are forgotten.

136

ARGUMENT

My college room mate has died,
And I remember
Our old discussion
About whether there were ghosts.
Now, I say to her, Now is the time
For you to win the argument
And prove you were right.

Or is the gulf fixed, after all,
Too wide? I would be glad
To have been mistaken.

137

THE OARSMAN

I still think of death, sometimes,
As I did when I was a child,
As the oarsman coming
With dripping oar
To row us all over
The sleepy water.
Some time, in the dark night,
In a half dream,
I may wake and go to sleep again
Drifting in the boat,
Hearing the slow splash
And hoping to wake up
Near the land
With familiar muffled figures
Gliding shadowy down to meet me
In the cool light.
Some time
There will be more figures
There than here.

Explorations

EAST COAST—CANADA

Lying at night poised between sleep and waking
Here on the continent's edge, I feel the wind shaking
The house and passing on:
Blowing from far across mountain ranges,
Far over the long sweep of the prairies,
Blowing from England over swelling seas,
Blowing up from the populous south.

The wind travels where we cannot travel,
Touches those we cannot touch;
For few and lonely are the sentinel cities of the North
And rivers and woods lie between.
Far, few, and lonely....

Space surrounds us, flows around us, drowns us.
Even when we meet each other, space flows between.
Our eyes glaze with distance.
Vast tracts of Arctic ice enclose our adjectives.
Our spirits are sheer columns of ice like frozen fountains
Dashed against by the wind.

Drown it out. Drown out the wind.
Turn on the radio.
Listen to the news.
Listen to a baseball game.
Pretend we belong to a civilization, even a dying one
Pretend. Pretend.

But there are the woods and the rivers and the wind blowing.
There is the sea. Space. The wind blowing.

ROADS

It was one night when we lived at the farm he came.
We were sitting playing dominoes at the kitchen table,
And the dominoes made roads along the oilcloth:
This road leads to Spain, I said;
That road is a Roman road.
The light from the kerosene lamp
Lay dim and yellow on the cracks in the floor.
They were roads, too, but they went nowhere.

He came in from the snow and darkness outside
Bringing the cold in with him for a minute,
Till Mother had replaced the old overcoat
That lay in front of the door to keep the draught out.
He was a stocky man, not young or old,
His black hair greying a little;
His mackinaw was mended, not ragged.

He wanted supper, so we took off the dominoes,
And Sister told me to bring a plate from the pantry,
And I stood by and watched it being filled.
He had come, he said, from Annapolis, had walked to
British Columbia,
And now he was walking home again, because
There was no work anywhere on the way.

I wonder now about that man, and whether
He ever reached home, or stayed home when he got there;
Whether he found what he wanted in Annapolis
Or turned and walked to west or south again.
I see him walking down dark roads in the rain,
Muddy roads, dusty roads, wet lengths of pavement
Blurrily reflecting the pointed edges of stars,
Lonely roads with burned woods on each side,
Wide roads becoming the streets of cities,
All mazily criss-crossing forever,
Turning and winding and doubling again forever,
Leading home and leading away from home,
But mostly leading nowhere.

COACH CLASS

Now the train,
Swaying towards the sunset, moves immense,
A wheezing monster. In the gathering dusk
I glimpse through fly-specked windows ragged children
Sitting on doorsteps staring with grave eyes...
A barking dog...boys playing ball, lithe-muscled....
And suddenly, at a crossing, a pallid face,
Gleaming up strangely among clustering moths,
And lost at once in darkness, to be vainly sought for....

Night settles down, and the bored travellers turn
From the empty dark to the empty brightness of novels,
Or eat ham sandwiches with listless hunger
And scatter candy wrappings on the floor.
A baby cries.... Two sailors quarrel loudly....
The man in the egg-stained suit
Snores, handkerchief over eyes,
And his wife pulls his topcoat round her shoulders....

The train jerks to a halt, and the sleepers, dazed,
Sit up, stretch, yawn, blink drowsiness from their lashes.
Another train moves past them, and they watch
The unconscious inhabitants of this new-found planet
Sitting in dazzling light. In the reflecting faces
They see themselves as suave and seasoned travellers,
Adventurers in strange lands. They sit erect,
Casual but gallant; then they plunge on,
Feeling space sliding from beneath their world.

LONDON FOG

Fog lies in the trees like pools of pale water,
Washing the new leaves, dripping on the sickly daffodils;
Fog wraps its damp and woolly scarf
Around the bent necks of the citizens,
Gets a stranglehold.
Fog is a smoke in the nostrils,
A grimy hand-print on the window pane.
Fog is a poison gas blurring out the pale faces of the children.

And among these children—
Condemned ghosts wandering in shades of underground—
And among these rickety and blurred tenements,
Among the dingy grocery shops where men in once-white
    aprons wait on tired women standing in queues,
Among the butcher shops where limp rabbits hang in unsightly
    death—
Among all these I wander,
Thinking of a high, frosty sky above white snow
And of green pines standing
Frosted by stillness
In a clear blue light.

143

LANDSCAPE FROM TRAIN WINDOW

From a train in the industrial North
(Not picture postcard England)
I watch the houses, identical Siamese twins,
Row on row, all dingily the same,
Heavy, sooty, washed in smoke-tasting fog
And a drizzle which is half dirt.

Opposite me there sits a stolid man
With a red face and pale, suspicious eyes,
And his young wife, newly married,
Nervously sipping the beer that he has bought her.
As we come into something approaching countryside
(Though still wrapped in the gray town smog)
She nudges him and points
Through the blurred window
At a brown patch of ground.
"Look," she says, "Look,
A cow in a field."

WINTER FEVER

Oh, I am restless, restless.
I wander through the rooms,
Pick up a book and drop it,
Wonder if I should write
A letter or a poem.

I'll write a letter of application
For a job in Florida
Where there is sunshine in February
Or maybe Alberta, where I can see the mountains
And there is not this flat marsh
With snow drifting on it.

I'll sell all my furniture—
Desks, bookcases, chairs—
All this useless clutter
That I dream at night
Lies heavy on my chest
And pins me down; and I'll buy a ticket
To fly TCA
And look down on the toylike
Absurd countryside.

But then I see myself
In Edmonton or Tallahassee
Shopping for desks, chairs, tables,
Rearranging life
In the same pattern
Only to want to break it
Over and over again;
And I wonder if it's worth while
To sell a desk with four drawers
To buy one with six.

VOYAGE

I have sailed my ship
Through Polar seas
Past stony shores,
Bleak fastnesses

Where white ice breaks
against grey stone;
Past icebergs sailing,
Grand, alone

Against a pale
And frosty sky
Into a cold
Infinity.

O, bring me, winds
More soft and fair
To where those pleasant
Pastures are,

146

Green with spring rains
And peaceful sun,
Where streams in thousand
Branches run.

There shepherds play
Their pipes and sing,
With shepherdesses
Gossiping,

And children
Underneath the trees
Pick blossoms of
Wild Strawberries,

And never breath
From Polar sky
Freezes their blood
Ungraciously.

147

TOBIAS AND THE ANGEL

Tobias, with the angel and his dog,
Set off upon his journey. His blind father
Had sent him with his blessing on his way.
It was hot weather, and the dog ran panting,
His pink tongue lolling, sniffing at the road.
Tobias whistled to him, hummed a tune,
Dreamed of strange cities tapering to the sky.
What villages, what fields, what woods, what pastures,
What farm houses where girls with sunny hair
Stood combing it before their open doors
He yet might pass before he reached the city
Where he could claim the debt owed to his father?

In the evening they made camp beside the river,
And the young Tobias from his knapsack drew
The food old Anna had prepared. On a grassy bank
He and the angel lazed, watching the fireflies
Dancing their mazy dance, and talked at length
Of journeys and the ways to undertake them.

Later, Tobias, swimming in the river,
Raced with the angel. The cool water sprayed
About their heads and made a moonlit halo.
The dog swam after them, snorting with joy.

148

And then the fish appeared, the magic beast,
Silently cutting through the silver waves,
And with his huge mouth opened greedily
Bore down upon Tobias. Terrified,
Tobias waited to be swallowed up.
But then the angel cried to him, "Tobias,
Take him by the gill and pull him to dry land."
And so he did, and there the great fish lay,
Panting upon the bank, the very brother
Of Jonas's old friend and host. The dog
Nosed at his dying length, but turned away.

And even Tobias, staring, could not know
This was the magic flesh would feed his journey,
The antidote against the evil spell
Upon his bride, salve for his father's blindness.
Cutting the fish's heart out, he stood still
And turned it over in his puzzled hands.
And there he held the journey and its end,
His gay return, leading his bride and treasure,
To his mother watching eager from her window
And his father stumbling to the door with his cane,
While the dog ran barking into the front yard.

149

THE ANGEL SPEAKS TO TOBIAS

Fear not the mighty monster from the deep
Though he strive to kill you.
Struggle to bring him to dry land.
His flesh will heal you
Of all the evils that
To man or woman come,
The blinded eye,
The barren womb.

Like Jacob with the angel, strive with him.
Rip out his heart,
His liver, gall, and entrails. Find his name
Traced on each part.

His heart shall drive away
All evil spells.
Burn it, and by its flame you'll sea
What virtue in it dwells.

150

Devotions

PEACE: I

Peace is what is found
When the sailor sets his will
To turn from a rough sea
To a rougher still.

Peace is a walking out
From a cold room
Into a colder blizzard
And drifted doom.

Peace is pain increased
Till it is numb,
And a cry so shrill
That it seems dumb.

Peace cannot be shaken
By death or strife,
For it has swallowed both
To make its life.

151

PEACE: II

Grant us thy peace, O God;
Not peace of frozen sod,
Or icicles that shine
Tidily in a line;
Not peace of rigid stone,
Monument to cold bone,

But peace of the warm earth
That mothers each new birth
Of grass-blade or of lamb,
And gives them all a home;

Peace of the growing rose
Unfolding to disclose
New joys and ever-new
To catch the observer's view;

Of birds that soar and sing
From pastures blossoming,
And drop from joyous throats
Their sweet and tranquil notes.

Oh, not in snow may come
Our absolution,
But water flowing free
To all eternity,
That with its fertile waves
Makes garden-plots of graves.

SUPPOSITION

Just for a moment, suppose that it were true,
That miracles were possible, even for oneself,
That the Holy Dove might actually descend.
Suppose that the God present in the wafer,
Swallowed like a seed, might spread his branches out,
A flourishing tree, putting forth virtues like leaves
And graces like fruit; suppose our guardian angel
Truly stands by us with his upraised wings
To protect us against the crowned and cruel arch-demon,
The evil enchanter with his wicked wand
Who casts his spell over our souls, poor birds
Caught in an eternal trap.

        Suppose that we're upheld
By the endless murmurs of prayer rising in swelling waves,
Gathered from the lonely, lost places of all the world
And having their sources in forgotten centuries.
Suppose that the lost voices of dead saints,
Mixing like incense with our own petitions,
Float them more gently to the gates of heaven.

Suppose, just for a moment, that God is real,
That, at the heart of this world where beauty walks with terror,
Where goodness and treachery are so strangely mixed,
There is goodness that is not ugly and beauty that is not cruel,
And peace that is true beyond all understanding.

Suppose this much to be true, and build upon it,
And hope what seems like sand may turn to rock.

POEM TO THE BLESSED VIRGIN

Lady, I come to light
A candle in your sight.
So frail this flame, like faith,
That wavers at a breath,
Yet scoops from darkest space
A place of light and peace.

Oh, frail this candle's flame,
Frail every human name,
And frail and delicate
The flesh that worms will eat;

Yet from your flesh was made
God, when he came to aid
With his divine nature
His lost and fallen creature.

You shielded in your arms
Heaven himself from harm,
And soothed his baby cries
With tender lullabies.

Children, to you we run.
Pray to your little son
Whom you so softly hold
To save us from the cold
Of our own bitterness
By means of his dear grace,
Who made the heaven and earth
But chose a human birth.

Honouring you, he chose
To honour us (his foes,
As we had else become
Who madly loved our doom)

And gave to flesh and blood
A glory not allowed
To spirits, though they flame
With an angelic name.

Your womb, the marriage bed
Where earth and heaven were wed,
Brings forth perpetually
Our life, even when we die.

Lady, my candle's light
Will die in the deep night.
Protect my soul's frail spark,
Wavering in the dark;
And all these others too,
Light with serener glow.
Pray for us, Lady, who
Have lit our lights for you.

155

ON A PAINTING OF THE ASSUMPTION

The metal haloes of the apostles shine
Above the lilied tomb; one figure bows
In grief, not seeing the vision; others lift
Rapt wooden faces to her downturned face,
The Mother of God, with grave, inscrutable smile
Dropping her blessings in a silken skein
To Thomas's doubting hand, while on each side
Angels with folded palms and peacock wings
Tidily guard her with their ordered ranks.

Motionless, midway between earth and heaven,
Against the glazed bright fabric of the sky,
She stands, and brings their tableau to her centre.
She is their moon, who draws their tidal gaze
While they stand still, a frozen continent,
Devotion hardening round them like a mould.

THE MILDNESS OF JESUS

Was Jesus so mild
As some have said?
He who called brimstone down
On the judged head,

Withered the fig tree
And blasted its root
That would not yield to him
Its early fruit?

Bethsaida, Chorazin
Knew the sound of his curse,
And the traders in the temple
The blows from his cords.

Kind he was as lightning
That strikes the rotten tree,
And loving as the fire that burns
The plague-filled city.

157

POEM FOR GOOD FRIDAY

O Holy cross,
O gracious tree
That casts so sweet a shade
On me,

Once you grew tall
In a green wood;
Rustling in new green leaves
You stood.

They chopped you down
Where tall you grew;
Birds from your frightened
Branches flew.
Two plain brown boards
They made of you.

Yet what green leaves
Could round you twine
More gently than this
Sacred Vine?

What fresher flowers
Could grace your wood
Than rosy blossoms
Of His blood?

What fruit more Eden-sweet
Could be
Than this dear flesh
That died for me?

158

POEM FOR THE YEAR OF FAITH

Faith is not less faith because it fluctuates,
Even in the presence of God,
And I think it must have been hard to believe
On the day of the Crucifixion.
I imagine the Man with a dark, plain face,
Dominated by the great nose, the brown eyes
Of an anonymous sufferer I once saw
In a movie of one of Hitler's Camps.
A little past his prime (as a man in his thirties would be then),
No wonder he stumbled under the wooden weight
Of the great cross. But would a God stumble?
His followers must have wondered.
Had Judas' kiss been needed
To show which of these men claimed to be God?

And his Mother standing there to watch the hanging,
A stout, greying woman in her fifties,
This good Jewish matron taken from her kitchen
And her concern for a neighbour's wedding or childbirth,
Could she be the Mother of Sorrows and of God
Whose "Yes" to the Spirit had brought God to the world?
Could doubting Thomas and denying Peter
And that other Mary
(Neurotic, or disreputable, or both)
From whom the devils had been cast,
And the handful of disciples who were always wrong,
Always clumsy, always being rebuked
And getting into disputes about who was greatest—
Could they see visions, perform miracles,
Be saints and martyrs, found the Church of Christ?
It seems, indeed, they could.

Well, but they saw the Christ transfigured,
Or raised from the dead and eating fish and honeycomb.
They touched their hands to the still open wounds.

But if they had wished to deny, even so,
Would they have been convinced?
Executioners bungle; men have escaped the hangman
(A while, anyhow) and lived to tell the tale.

Was their faith, in the long run, different from ours,
Who still struggle with this strange, this harsh, this gentle
Man who was either God, or mad, or a trickster,
But must be God?
His words tantalize the doubting ear:
  "I am the Way."
  "I am the Vine."
  "I am the Bread of Life."
  "I have overcome the world."
  "I and the Father are one."
  "Come unto me."
  "I am with you always."
  "I am Jesus, whom you persecute."

And indeed the Presence is still here,
Tangible (sometimes) as the wounds were to Thomas.
It is not surprising that we sometimes forget,
That the Presence sometimes withdraws and is remote.
Perhaps there were days later when Thomas wondered
If he had really touched and seen, or if his memory
Was maybe playing tricks.
All he could do then was to do
As we still must,
Remember there were other witnesses,
Remember that we saw, will see again,
And wait, and wait.

END OF THE WORLD

At eight years old
On a summer evening
With the scarlet runner in flower
And the smell of heat in the air
I read for the first time
The Revelation of St. John
And yearned
For the end of the world
For the sea of glass
The angels holding the four winds
The woman clothed with the sun
Flying on eagle wings
Whose child should conquer
The great dragon.

And still I hope
(O Mother dear Jerusalem)
Hearing someone say
That Billy Graham prophesies the End
And having read the directions
For survival in emergencies
And knowing I could not survive
And knowing I will never hold a ban-the-bomb placard
As I could not have killed the guards
On the way to the gas chambers
Being of those who walk
In a quiet and orderly manner
To their own funerals

And still I hope
(In spite of the fact
That there was much to be said for Babylon
And it has said much for itself
And indeed I have loved it
As much as I have hated it
And would save it if I could)

For the great dream city
Beyond destruction
Which our fathers loved better than life
Where the dead live forever
In air pure as fire
And cool as water
And there is no night
And no injustice
And no loneliness
And no death
And no bombs
And no tombs
No riots
No tear gas
And no tears
Because they have all been wept long ago.
There will be no more tears.

Pilgrims

WILLIAM BREWSTER DISEMBARKING
FROM THE *MAYFLOWER*

We sailed in September,
A hundred and two of us
Crowded on one ship
After the *Speedwell* had been sent back,
Unseaworthy vessel. We first had good weather.
There was some quarrelling: We were not all Saints,
And even Saints do not always agree.
All plain men we were, though;
None, thank God, with pride of blood
Or family tree; Sons of Adam:
James Chilton, tailor, of Canterbury;
Sam Eaton, of Bristol, ship's carpenter,
With his wife Sarah and a sucking child;
Grave Richard Warren, a useful instrument;
Myles Standish, a good soldier;
The Billingtons of London, a most profane family
(Doomed to be hanged, no doubt);
My own wife Mary,
My sons Love and Wrestling
(Jonathan left in Leyden
With Fear and Patience,
His young sisters).

The trip seemed long, the quarters narrow.
We tired of our diet of salt horse and hardtack.
The weather worsened. Many were seasick.
Stink of slop and vomit tainted the air,
And smell of unwashed bodies
Crowded below deck.

The sailors (not Saints) swore at the sick.
But the hand of God struck one profane young man. He died
  and was buried
In the swelling sea.
But Saints died too. Young William Butten,
Deacon Fuller's servant, died in November.

On the tenth of November,
After a long tossing,
The lookout at dawn cried "Land ahoy!"
And, not a little joyful, we crowded to the rails.
But we were nearly lost
In the treacherous water.
All night we lay at sea, and finally entered
This good harbour.

We have still much to fear:
Mutiny, hunger, cold, hostile natives,
Dissension among ourselves, a savage life
In a strange country.

We must not be homesick
For the flat fens of Lincolnshire
And its farmhouses dark with age,
Nor for London streets, or Amsterdam,
No, nor for Leyden, that goodly city
Where we lived twelve years.
For we are Pilgrims
Who seek a City
Beyond all earthly seas and bounds of space
Where no waves break and God is Governor.

GEORGE CRABBE

He planted weeds, not flowers, in his garden;
Collected shells and fossils; observed fish;
Observed humans also with a cool eye,
And of the conscience he was scientist.

Not the beautiful intrigued him, not the virtuous,
The noble peasant or the dashing devil,
But the parish clerk turned thief, the seedy coquette,
The merchant with just half a mind to evil.

He deplored extremes, disliked the Methodists
And Deists also; was wary of romance:
Yet took opium; noted down his dreams;
Fell in love at sixty; and, homesick, once
Rode his horse all day to reach the ocean,
Plunged in its waves, and then rode back again.

165

KEATS AT ROME

Death was not easeful to him at the end,
Coughing up blood and sputum, lungs half gone,
Poor and a stranger in a foreign town,
Without a relative or dearer friend

Than plaintive, timid Severn close at hand.
Even the mighty dead whose words had grown
So dear to him had left him all alone,
Their sunlike glory faded. He could spend

Scarcely a sigh on them or on his fame.
Only a distant sound, like golden bees
Swinging and singing on lost summer air,
Grew till he woke from Homer's distant seas
To waters moving dark and thick as dream,
And death's long solemn roar crashed on his ear.

166

CARDINAL NEWMAN

Not peace, but holiness. That was the light
Toward which his soul yearned. Walking delicately
On the knife edge of controversy he discovered faith
At the end of the blade. The *via media*
After all was not for him. Better too much
Than too little, especially of faith.

The true church must be that which the wise disdained,
Should appear even superstitious, should be slandered
As gross, dangerous, absurd, unchristian.
The virtues it maintained should be unfashionable,
Like humility, charity, chastity, faith.

For faith he must give up peace,
The snapdragons outside his rooms at Oxford,
The willowy tall spires, the familiar prayers,
His old friends. (Pusey told him,
"I think you should leave England.")

A convert, he noted, is not much trusted by anybody.
His new friends are cold, his old friends withdraw.
At best they say, "I suppose he must be sincere."

But in the kingdom of heaven there is no loss,
He told himself.
Take a city full of people, full of their separate plans,
Crowding the streets and shops,
Walking, riding in carriages;
Or take the authors you read in your room at Oxford,
Clustering mutely around your desk,
Those supposed to be dead and those now living:
Nothing will be lost, they will live forever,
Not just behind the curtains of your eyes, but in reality.

The pious child who yearned for the truth of miracles
And crossed himself on the threshold of dark rooms,
Who saw a heavenly light linger on his grandmother's breakfast
    things
Or on the field full of cowslips,
Grew up to kneel under faith's dark wings,
To be led by a pillar of light in lonely Sicily,
And to hear the voice of the beloved saying,
"This is indeed my body. Take, eat."

TO THE GHOST OF ERNEST DOWSON

Pale ghost, whose unrequited
Perfumed love makes moan
In songs of lutes and roses,
A dreaming monotone;

How decorative your passion,
How fanciful your grief,
How languorous the music
In which you found relief.

Pale, cold, and false your lady,
And pale and cold are you:
Yet true your melancholy,
Your bitter spleen is true.

D.H. LAWRENCE, PILGRIM

It would be easy to be ironic
About this saviour who could not save himself
Turning so eagerly toward life
His fretful, feverish, tubercular energy;
Easy for those who sit still amassing
Their small heaps of security
To deplore that restless wandering
From England to Italy to New Mexico
To Australia to Italy again
And finally (so early) to the world beyond all worlds.
It would be easy to say, Here was a man
Who praised friendship and was alienated from his friends,
Who praised love and quarrelled bitterly,
Who praised sex and had no children,
Who cried out against the world's debasement of man,
But could find no remedy
Except that men should wear red sashes
And dance in the streets.
And how mixed with nonsense his Gospel is,
And how easily distorted.

And yet, for all that, he wins over his detractors
By the pure force and beauty of flame flaring in darkness,
Life transitory but triumphant
Rippling like a gold snake from shadow to shadow
In the grim valley of death.

DAG HAMMARSKJOLD: NEAR MARTYR

An inward man, self torturing,
He lived with the wish for death and the fear of death,
With dreams of drowning, head pushed under water,
Held by an act of will;
Dreams of dizziness on cliffs in a mountainous country,
Cold and high;
Dreams of facing an execution squad
In a shabby courtyard with no companions.

Yet, though he intended to choose the Way of the Cross,
Gethsemane, rather than Calvary, was his home:
The vigil while others slept,
The dark garden, silence, the sense of desertion,
"Wilderness for his pillow, a star for his brother."

His death itself was release rather than martyrdom,
The accident, the whim of the 'plane's plunging,
The solemn fall through space
To find again beyond the humid jungle
The cold, remote country of his dreams,
Waterfalls falling like mist,
Arctic blossoms delicate as waterfalls;
The walk through that air so light for breathing
Into a world as strange as dawn or moonlight
By far lakes, or at the ocean's verge,
Alone, happy, purged of the world's guilt.

The unicorn is not abnormal
Because it has no mate.

ANSWER TO A POEM ON SAINT JOHN
BY RAYMOND SOUSTER

No, there are no longer street cars
Running up from the harbour,
Over which, however,
The gulls still fly.
Today, the water is blue
And the sky pale blue, cloudless.
The August morning sparkles
On the verge of autumn,
Fresh and cold.
Above the harbour, the church spire
Rises, surrounded by staging:
They are repairing the clock tower.
In front of the hotel
There is still confetti
From yesterday's wedding reception.
Next door
People are coming out of
The Full Gospel Assembly,
Sunday saved.

171

In King Square
The benches are crowded
With loafers and lovers
And a few tourists,
And there are pigeons
And a sparkling fountain
As there are in most squares,
And the children
(As in most squares)
Feed the pigeons
And watch the fountain
While the adults
Watch the children watching.
The statue of Tilley still stands
Pigeon spattered,
But you may not remember
The skater on stone skates
Or the memorial to
Our Glorious Dead, 1939 dash 1945.

Perhaps the stench of poverty
Is not as strong as it was
When you were here
(Anyhow, obviously
It's a finer day
This cool, bright Sunday)

But there is a smell
Like sour glue
From the pulp and paper factory
Mixed with the salt smell of sea.

Poems for All Seasons

VALLEY BY 'BUS: NOVEMBER

The familiar landscape
Appears through the mist
As foreign,
Chinese.
The river is grey silk.
The trees are picture language
Written on the sky,
A bare alphabet.
Rocks, barns, mail boxes
Are matching grey.
A watery sun reveals
Brown, curled ferns,
A spray of amber leaves,
A sudden field
Wet and green as spring
Against the brown.

173

AFTERNOON SNOW

Snow falls
From the white-grey sky
Soft and weary;
Snow falls, and my heart is sad.
I have closed my room from the weather;
I have bought chrysanthemums,
Small yellow suns in the winter room;
But snow falls, and the world is wrapped in grey.
The afternoon lengthens and grows dim.
My eyes are giddy from watching the window.
I want you to come, and am afraid you may.
You might walk past, in the soft dark street,
And I would never know.

TWO MINDS

Why am I embarrassed,
Wordless, or speaking words that don't matter,
Breathless, my mouth dry,
My hands trembling a little,
As I pour you a cup of tea?
Do I wish or fear your touch,
Reaching out my own hand blindly
To fondle the soft heads of the chrysanthemums
In the vase by my side,
To stroke their long green stems?

AFTERNOON AT CURRIE'S MOUNTAIN

The April afternoon
Is still and sweet.
Limp and winter-white,
We lie in the moist heat,

And feel the searching sun
Counting our bones
With cold-hot touch.
We might be sticks or stones,

Or last year's leaves,
Or needles fallen down
From pines that stir above,
Remote and green.

How good to be like ferns
Or roots of trees
Whose branches grow entwined
In forest silences,

Not separated by
The cold dividing mind,
Conscience, or cowardice,
Or the tongue's wound,

But leaning close, without
Word, or sigh, or moan,
Sentient but motionless,
In the renewing sun.

175

MAY EVENING

In the spring
I feel life ebbing from me.
May is so beautiful
I could cry that it will not last
That these pale yellow leaves
These dandelions on roadsides
Anemones on the edge of woods
The air so cool so fresh
So perfumed
The washed blue sky
Children's voices
Will not last
There is no way of keeping them.
Oh, I could cry
For all the Mays gone past
That will never come again
And for those that will come yet
When I am too old to weep for them
Or have become clay
My folded hands
Crumbling
Crumbled
Unable to feel the touch of grass
Or of other hands.

SUMMER SADNESS

I wonder why June evenings
Seem so much sadder than those in winter.
Is it because the prolonged half light
Makes me restless,
So that I think I could walk to the rim of dusk,
And I understand cyclists
In pursuit of speed and violence?
Is it because all this greenery
All this flowering forth
Causes me to remember and protest
My own lack of flowering?
Is it because the wind of early summer
Moving in all the leaves of all the maples
Troubles me with longing
For some touch more delicately painful
Than I have ever known
Or am likely to know?

Winter will come soon enough.
Then I can close my windows,
Draw my drapes,
Turn on my reading lamp,
And sit quietly reading the evening paper.
The weather outside will not matter,
And if the wind blows
Across the zero snow
And through bare branches
I do not intend to hear it.

177

SUMMER EVENING AT JOGGINS

Fundy wrinkles as soft as an inland river
With a sullen sound of spray in the sunset distance.
Here are life's beginnings, in this salt tide
That has cut these harsh cliffs to forbidding shapes,
Slimed the rolled-over stones with green seaweed,
Covered the shores with barnacles, snails, dogwhelks that eat
    the snails.
The air is dank with the smell of life and dying life,
Water and salt and stone.

On this beach you may clamber rocks enclosing
The fossil prints of tree trunks dead for centuries,
Like a dead leaf pressed at random in a book;
And, still alive upon this corpse of life
(Symbol of all life which finds sustenance
In strange, grey ways) you find
The shelled limpet clinging
With soft foot to hard stone.

HEAT WAVE

How tired the maple
Outside my window
With its leaves moving faintly
And the listless birds cheeping in it.
How tired the voices of the children
Teasing the dog across the street
As a truck drives past
To dampen the pavement.
How tired the peonies
Pale pink, full blown,
Drooping their heads
Over the lip of my blue jug,
Scattering a few petals.
How tired I am
In the hot, moist morning
Walking about the room in bare feet,
Standing at the door
For a breath of cool air.

AUGUST AFTERNOON

Summer is almost over now. The fountain
Still sprays its untired coolness on the grass,
And grass is lush, and clover what it was,
And ducks still move like squadrons in formation,
Stepping downward to the water's brink. They paddle
As young as ever on the waves. And yet
One's lame now. Something's happened to his foot.
Ducks and ourselves are not as fit as fiddles.

Fall's not in air; frost has not hit the leaves;
But the marsh smells of blackberries and hay.
The goldenrod waves thick; the jewel weed
Winds its small orange horn powdered with red.
Cling to this sunshine, pile the summer day
Close pressed for winter under mind's dark eaves.

GLADIOLI

Never again the green world
Of Spring
Or the first light of dawn,
With dew
Weighing the dandelions,
Cobwebs fine and sparkling
On the grass;
Never again the child
Dazed with newness
And the mist of colour
Breathing the dark scent
Of the moist April soil.
Sun has burned too long
For early blossoms.
Nothing is left but August
And the dusky
Glowing
Gladioli
Like spikes of flame.

181

THIS IS NONE OF ME

Awakening suddenly in the night
I am not sure at first where I am.
I've missed my 'plane, I think:
I'm still in London.
I must have fallen asleep in the afternoon,
And now it's dark outside.
But the room is bigger than I remember,
And why, I wonder, is the door open?
I sit up, and try to find my glasses,
But the bedside table is on the wrong side.
Fortunately the drapes aren't drawn,
And a beam of light from a streetlight
Reveals the dressing table with a mirror over it.

I leap up, stumble over my suitcase on the floor,
And see my desk with the typewriter on top
While my hand finds a chair-top.
After all, when I turn on the lights,
I am at home.
Everything has become familiar.
I did catch the 'plane.
With memory returning,
I feel the floor as solid.
I see myself in the mirror, looking frightened,
And begin to laugh at myself.
Outside, a motorcycle roaring past
Is no longer part of foreign traffic
But a homely local sound.

Turning off the lamp, I lie down again,
Press my face in the pillow, and breathe the night,
The still, hot darkness of July.
On the other side of the Atlantic,
In the room where I thought I was sleeping,
Some other tourist wakes with dawn
And wonders for a moment where he is.
The spinning world
Creates the seasons of our minds,
Unites our dreams.

SAINT JOHN RIVER IN OCTOBER

It is late afternoon
In mid-October.
The smell of brittle leaves
Is in the air.
I walk by the river
By which I have walked many times
And I remember
All those autumns
And all those springs smelling of lilacs
And I remember when I was nineteen
And thinking
"I have never been so sad,"
Or "I have never been so happy,"
As the case might be.
I remember being kissed for the first time
On a park bench on a September evening
With the lights colouring the dark water;
And I remember sitting alone crying
Because someone had crossed the street
Without speaking to me.

I remember talking to an old woman
Who had moved away and come back again
So she could die in a house near the river.
I remember seeing the ice go out of the river,
The white bobbing cakes against dark blue;
And summers with regattas,
And band concerts on the Green,
And children swimming.
I remember V-E day
And people walking
With toy flags by the river.

And I am surprised that all that time has gone,
That life has flowed away with the river,
And all the tears, humiliations, hopes, quarrels
Have gone into the soil like the dead leaves
To be buried under another winter's snow
Or feed the roots of next spring's pussywillows.

SUNRISE NORTH

RISING FROM WINNIPEG

Rising from Winnipeg
we see the houses
pink and blue match boxes beneath us
and then the land
an abstract painting
in green and yellow squares,
the roads like rulers

And up we rise
through miles of white fog
to a glimpse of sky
with clouds beneath us
foamy as detergent
on a washday.

We are poised over sky
as though it were the sea
blue, spray-tossed;
and on the far edge
are white icebergs
motionless
over which the plane
seems to stand still.

Now they have disappeared
and the foam is solid
so that you think you could step
from the plane window
and snowshoe over
a field of drifted white.

A woman sits opposite
sipping lemonade
and eating a cherry
on the end of a stick.

MOVING DAY

I sit on the floor
of my living room
which is furnished
only by a telephone
and look out the drapeless windows
at the city below
the rows of houses
with peaked roofs
of many colours
the other apartment buildings
the domed roof of the Ukrainian church
streets with cars
and people walking.

There will be a chair in that corner,
I think,
and above it a painting
of red on blue.
There will be books
and on the desk over there
which is not yet over there
I shall put a vase for chrysanthemums
or for the first daffodils of next April.

I have not yet decided
how I shall arrange
my visitors.

187

DWARF HIGHRISE

From this angle
the apartment building
looks pie-shaped
though I know it is a rectangle.
Also it is small, made with a child's blocks—
no, made with dominoes heaped up,
a black slab of wall with dots of light.

Inside are people
also small,
so small I can't see them.
They walk around behind the lighted dots,
fiddle with the minute knobs
of toy television sets.

They cook, eat, make love, do pushups
with precise cardboard motions.

Maybe someone has even
taken a sheet of paper
from a doll's house desk
and sits imagining

a Lilliputian poem
smaller than a speck.

AUTUMN HAIKU

1

Outside my window
grey sky, and the top of a tree
blowing in the wind

2

The birds are flying
in flocks towards the south:
an airplane also flies.

3

A white paper half moon
hangs low, a kite falling
from the five o'clock sky.

4

The pines are still green
among the yellow leaves of autumn:
I think of you.

5

The lights of the city
begin to appear. Now
the time of short days begins.

POEM WRITTEN IN ABSENCE

Resting in my living room
in half darkness
tired after the day's work
I drowse and watch the lights of the city
stretch in long yellow rows
under a purple sky.

Below me I hear cars hum distantly
and somebody typing
too far off
to disturb.

Now in this quiet time
I wish you were with me,
maybe not talking,
maybe not even touching,
but just being here
in the gentle dusk.

Even imagining you
in the room
fills me with a sense
of such strength and sweetness
that I cannot really be lonely
thinking of you.

WIND

My father
would have loathed this place.
He hated wind,
and although I don't mind it myself
I think of him
and shiver.

COLD SPELL

Today, walking the zero street,
I know I am alive because the wind cuts
my open cheek; my scarf scratches my throat.
The passers-by wear fur and wool
thick thick.
I meet a little girl and her mother,
the child holding mittens to her face
to warm it.
Frost sparkles on the roofs of the small kiosks
at street corners
and on the red berries of the mountain ash
outside the apartment building.

191

I come in
ride up in the hot elevator
to the twelfth floor
take off snow boots
fling coat, fur bonnet on the bed
stand by my window
pushing aside drapes to see
again from above
the snowy roofs
the smoke from chimneys
the slow cars
pedestrians huddled shivering.

What is the weather now in your country?
I would like to be a magician
who, by gazing through my window,
could bring you
from wherever you were
into this cold landscape.
Suddenly you would appear walking
past that house with the blue roof
and up over the black pines
towards my window.
When you came in
I would have to warm
your cold hands with mine.

192

SIGN LANGUAGE

Can words comfort
as the body comforts
or the mind understand
as flesh understands?

Your written words wound me
and I cannot reach you with mine,
but tenderness would flow
from the tips of my fingers
into yours
if you were with me.

In a world of separation
and silences,
why should it not be allowable
for the deaf and dumb
to speak with their fingers?

193

SUNRISE NORTH

Drawing my drapes, I see
pink and purple clouds of dawn
over the white-roofed city,
smoke in rising fountains,
the lights of early risers
twinkling far off,
the new moon, hanging low,
beginning to pale in the morning sky.

The beautiful northern city
is a child's Christmas toy
spread out like blocks
with here and there a tree
deftly placed
discreetly frosted;
and, like a child,
I want to pick it up,
move a house here, a tree there,
put more frost on that distant dome.

The colours fade, the pale blue sky grows higher.
Now I see the sun
gradually rising
over the rim of water-flat plain,
bonfire bright, triumphant.
Soon I shall walk out,
through the white snow, dry as sugar,
into the real street.

SUNDAY MORNING

It is twenty below outside
and something has happened to the church's heating.
The congregation sits
heavy coated
huddled in scarves, fur hats,
hands in pockets.
The man in front of me
sneezes and shivers.

It is no special day.
Christmas is over,
Lent has not yet started.
It is a long time
to any time.
The priest wears green
for hope.
In January
green is a cold colour.
His hands look cold.

195

Luckily, there is no sermon.
The choir sings
coldly
Rise up, O men of God
and we rise up.

Outdoors the weather is grey.
Snow falls a little,
and a yellow snow plough
is coming up the street.
A small boy, darting from his mother
and running with arms outstretched,
calls out
"Look at me
look at me.
I am a kite
blowing in the wind."

196

SELF-RELIANCE: TO RALPH WALDO EMERSON

Ralph Waldo, I remember I didn't like you
when I first read you. You were always in limp leather
or imitation leather, intended for gifts;
and you were full of wise saws
too suitable for quotation.
I thought you cold
for wanting your friends' company
only when it suited you.

But now as I sit at my kitchen table
with a cup of coffee at my elbow
and your essays in front of me
(Because I have taken them from the shelf with my eyes closed
asking the aid of Providence and the stars)
I think the wisdom after all is genuine.
Your plain New England wit
wears well; your stubborn honesty
refusing to be philanthropic,
to feign concern,
to give love or money to those
for whom you did not care;
your self-reliance.

197

Yes, you were right:
To be one's own wholly,
not to be swayed by this or that crowd
screaming "Hate, hate!"
or "Love, love!"
not to strive to be
like everyone else
(or unlike everyone else)—
that simple integrity
is the most difficult virtue
as much now as it was then.

Ralph Waldo, now I call your spirit up
at my convenience and not yours.
Your Yankee voice speaks
as I turn the page:
"The voyage of the best ship is a zigzag line."
"Isolation must precede society."
"I grieve that grief can teach me nothing."
"He that writes to himself
writes to an eternal public."

And so you do, Ralph Waldo.
I sit and stir the coffee in my cup.

THE FUTURE OF POETRY IN CANADA

Some people say we live in a modern mechanized nation
where the only places that matter
are Toronto, Montreal, and maybe Vancouver;
but I myself prefer Goodridge, Alberta,
a town where electricity arrived in 1953,
the telephone in 1963.

In Goodridge, Alberta
the most important social events
have been the golden wedding anniversaries of the residents.
There have been a Garden Club, a Junior Grain Club, and a
    Credit Union,
and there have been farewell parties,
well attended in spite of the blizzards.

Weather is important in Goodridge.
People remember the time they threshed in the snow,
and the winter the temperature fell to seventy below.

They also remember the time
the teacher from White Rat School
piled eight children in his car
and drove them, as a treat,
all the way to Edmonton;
where they admired the Jubilee Auditorium
and the Parliament Buildings
and visited the CNR wash rooms
but were especially thrilled
going up and down in an elevator.

I hope at least one poet
in the next generation
comes from Goodridge, Alberta.

IT MUST BE LOVELY TO WORK IN A LIBRARY

I sit in a room
with seventy people.
At one end of the room
searchers search cards
from Library of Congress catalogues
and photograph them.
Others sit changing
the blown-up photographs
so that they will fit our books.
Also there are some people
who type up direction slips
for books whose cards
cannot be found.
There are typists
typing cards
so that they can be multiplied,
and filers to file the cards
in the catalogue drawers,
which are then checked.

Up through the floors of stacks
the books are ranged
with tidy labels,
come down to be charged out
by an efficient
photographic method.

The dust of books
falls slowly,
seeps through the pores
of many minds.

It is always rewarding
To be part of a worthwhile enterprise.

LITTLE MAGAZINE

In the living room we sit arguing
about the new magazine.

It must be north
It must be west
It must be anywhere

Be (but definitely)
Canadian
but could have items on Scotland

illustrated with Eskimo prints

It must have
a central theme
not have a central theme

have one editor
be edited by a committee

contain only poems and stories
only criticism
criticism and some poems
critical poems

201

should be monthly
quarterly

daily?

mimeographed xeroxed
printed in Japan

should be done in cooperation with
the Drama Department
Fine Arts Department
Boreal Institute

but first of all
since the University has refused to pay
where (where in hell)
in Alberta
do we get the money?

202

TRAIN JOURNEY

All night the prairie like an inland sea
rolled past our window.
Sometimes, nodding awake,
we glimpsed a town receding,
six houses and a grain elevator;
and next day all day
there were woods rocks lakes waterfalls
and then waterfalls lakes rocks woods
with a few clearings
where snow lay in patches
or where violets grew
in a spot where no one would ever pick them.

Somewhere south and east were cities
towards which the train laboured,
and men had laid these tracks
running through granite.
But sometimes, looking out the window,
I wondered,
          Where are all those people
the world is supposed to be so full of?
Will cities creep like moss
over these boulders stained by time
set in unpopulated space?

CONVERSATION BETWEEN FRIENDS, LARGELY UNSPOKEN

A:
I grew up in a large house in a warm country.
A pomegranate tree stood in the courtyard.
The coconut's milk was sweet and cool
on summer days.
I was the youngest child of old parents.
My father spoiled me, my brothers petted me,
but there was no one near my age to talk to.
I talked to the trees.
I made friends with particular pebbles.

B:
I was my parents' only daughter.
In Estonia, in the days before the War,
we lived in a cold climate.
I stamped my feet on snowy ground
and saw my breath on the air
solid as feathers.

A:
I was a tomboy.
I liked playing in the rain
and swinging from branches.
I teased my elder sister,
who cried easily.
My mother and the maids
could not control me.

B:
I grew tall
and wore my pale hair in a braid.
I was clever at school, but melancholy.
My best friend killed herself
when she was only fifteen,
they said for love.

A:
I went to school and became more ladylike.
I stood upright at my desk
when I answered a teacher's question.
I was not allowed to cross my legs
or slouch when I walked
or laugh out loud.

B:
My country was occupied
first by Germans and then by Russians.
I disliked the Russians most.
My father died in a Russian work camp.
I became a refugee, and starved,
and was ill a long time,
and then scrubbed floors
and had a little more to eat, but not much more.
You do not know how I suffered.

205

A:
I did not suffer, but I was restless.
I wanted to be a dozen people,
to study philosophy and mathematics,
to take part in politics,
to write a novel and a cookbook.
I ran up and down stairways
singing.
Water from taps was not cold enough for me.
I ran to the well with a bucket
and poured it cold
over my long hair and tingling shoulders.

B:
I married, and was disappointed in marriage.
My husband lives in a distant city.
My daughter, however, is beautiful.
I lie awake nights and worry about her.

A:
My parents arranged my marriage, but it is happy.
I have not spent many nights away from my husband.
My son is tall, my daughter wears my sandals,
grey sprinkles my hair;
but still I run up and down stairways,
I put on flowered saris,
and remember myself under the pomegranate tree.
My horoscope foretells a long life.

DISPLACED PERSON

She was born in Russia, spent her youth in France,
now, at fifty,
lives in a basement apartment in a small town
in the American mid-West.
She has four cats
which take turns sitting on her shoulder
when she drinks a glass of hot tea.
"They have more courtesy," she says,
"than most of the people."

Her walls are covered
with maps instead of windows,
Russia or Greece or Egypt.
She wants to go to Mexico for the heat
and to Montreal
for the sake of the beautiful cold.

Meanwhile, sometimes she spends
a week-end in Chicago
or an evening watching a foreign movie,
or cooks exotic dinners
which the cats, having been born in Wisconsin
and brought up on milk and cat food,
do not always like.

HOLIDAY CAMPUS, LATE SUNDAY AFTERNOON

Here on the empty campus
deserted by students
there is no sign of life
except for one robin
moving as though on wheels
jerking its mechanical neck
up from tugging
a long brown worm
out of the ground.

It is like one of those dreams
one sometimes has
of walking through courtyards
past buildings where nobody lives,
a perfect reconstruction
of some ancient town
destroyed by a volcano
or a conquest.

A half-finished building
stands as though abandoned.
A sprinkler sprinkles
an untouched lawn.

The green trees swimming
in yellow sunshine
the lilac scent
this hushed peace
of suspended movement
begin to make me nervous,
and I move
away towards streets
where men mow lawns
and children play,
calling to each other
in high singsong voices.

SUNDAY AFTERNOON,
DOWNTOWN EDMONTON

Almost nobody stirs
in this concrete desert.
Sunshine burns
through the hot bright hazeless inland air
dazzles the eyes
and prickles the skin.
All the buildings look empty.
A few passers-by stare into windows;
a few policemen stand at street corners.
Men sit on shadeless benches
as though waiting for something to happen
which will probably never happen.
A dozen boys wait
for a bus which takes half an hour to come.
There is nothing to do,
and the afternoon is too hot
for doing nothing pleasurably.

FROM MY WESTERN WINDOW
(JULY 17, 1969)

Looking out of my western window
I see the new moon, balanced on its tip,
hanging just above the next apartment building.
Is this thin blade
really the same moon
towards which the three space travellers
now journey?

Now the moon hides
slid down behind the tower;
now it reappears
moving beyond the building
a dull orange glow
behind clouds.
Now it has gone completely.

The night is dark.
Many travellers speed
towards strange destinations.

TEA LEAF READING

The fortune teller is tired.
She has told too many fortunes.
This afternoon there have been
too many girls wanting husbands,
new jobs, adventure,
profitable journeys, inheritances.
"You are worried about a dark man,"
she has said to one; to another,
"Now is the time to sign the document.
You will live by the coast. You will marry
a wealthy man in a small town."

The fortune teller is fat
in a purple dress.
She is devout Greek Orthodox.
An icon on her wall once spoke to her
giving her good advice.
Sometimes she sees
one of her customers
appear to her in a vision.

Her family does not approve
her fortune telling
but all the same
she thinks it is a good thing
to tell that worried lady,
"The friend you lost will come back.
I see a white house, big,
with trees around it."

This afternoon, however,
the fortune teller is tired.
Obviously, her feet hurt, and sweat
stands out on her forehead.
She stirs the tea leaves
so as to get a better view.
"A small wedding, maybe, in the country?
A trip? Some money coming in?
I think what you need is a good rest
somewhere near water."

The fortune teller is tired.

WATERCOLOUR OF EDMONTON

Here is the city in watercolour.
It is composed of
cubes, curves, straight lines.
The time is evening (probably).
The time is summer.
The buildings are seen through mist.
The sky is
all purple and pale blue dots.
The trees are
green mushrooms
or balloons.
Grass is green
waves, edged by
watery pink lines.

At the far right
is the artist's signature
illegible.

REFLECTION

The chandelier is reflected
in the window pane,
so that its glass pendants
hang in mid-air
against the early evening sky
forming a new celestial object
unsupported
nearer than the moon
but not to be reached
by any astronaut,

or maybe just a flower
yellow centred
with transparent tassels
and no root.

LABOUR DAY WEEKEND

It is the last hot weekend
of the summer.
I have left my balcony
where the heat burned
and I viewed the far off
yellow fields
and the pale green trees
a little dusty
and just down the street
the Texaco sign
turning
and the people walking past
girls in slacks
a nun in long black stockings
a man in shorts with a racket
under one arm
cars and cars
coming and going.

I could not see
the hollyhocks in the gardens
but I knew they were there.

214

Now I am inside
have retreated to coolness
my rows of books
a winter painting
of snow on brown grass.
In here, in this dim light,
I do not need sunglasses.

After a year
I still miss you
turn sometimes towards
my homeward window.

Nevertheless, I will not deny
the hot blue life outside
the sweetness
of the late summer
late afternoon sun
to which
I intend to return
as soon as I have finished
this sentence.

INDIAN SUMMER

At noon I decided
(walking up the street to do my errands)
that I really loved you,
and immediately felt happy,
as though April
were here again.

Why, I wonder?
Because after all there's no future in it,
nothing but a few half hours
breathlessly stolen
of sweetest pain.

One maple on the lawn
(the others bare)
shines pale gold,
more beautiful than it ever was
in the spring.
Tomorrow it will have no leaves,
but for today only
it is solid sunshine.

WISH

For you, I wish I were young and beautiful,
that my hair like a dark fountain
sprayed down my back and was cool and scented,
that my eyes were no longer near-sighted
but shone like Orion and the Pleiades,
that my mouth tasted like vin rosé
and my throat was a white hollow
in which you might drown.
I wish my breasts were round and voluptuous,
that I was soft where I should be soft,
slim where I should be slim,
smooth where I should be smooth.

And yet it does not worry me
that you are not as young as you were twenty years ago,
that sometimes I see lines in your forehead.
I would like to stroke them away
with the tips of my fingers,
which I think would still feel young to you
if your eyes were closed.

217

SEPTEMBER TWILIGHT

Autumn has come again with yellow leaves.
Once more I am surprised that summer's over.
For a while the light is soft and unregretful.
I sit by my window
watching the passing cars.
Tonight I do not too much mind
that I am alone.

Love, do you fear as I do
the cold winds of winter,
the white weight of snow?

ON AWAKENING AT NIGHT

I awake at night
from restless dreams
and yearn for the comfort
of flesh on warm flesh
for your hands on my breasts
for your mouth
for your body on mine;

and I long for you
as I might long
for the flow of sunshine
or for water fountains
bursting in my hot mouth.

218

NOVEMBER SUNDAY

I awoke tired
having dreamed of you,
but I cannot remember the dream.

Beyond my window
beyond the city
there are fields
and the fields roll eastward.
I see in my mind
cars driving
the wide flat highways
towards home.

I wonder again, as always,
if I truly love you
or if only my breasts love you,
wanting your hand.

Can I analyse longing
or weigh desire,
dispel an illusion
by reducing it to so much chemistry,
an attraction of atoms for atoms?

I admit I do not understand you.

219

Nor do you understand me.
My mind has caves
secret and deep
and darkly shaded.
If you came in
you might be lost there
forever.
I also might be lost
exploring you,
might forget the boundaries
of my own selfhood.

To understand
and to be understood
and yet to be beloved
in spite of understanding
or because of it
is, I suppose,
what we all want.

Yet another person
is an island world
alien, dangerous.
All around the shores
are piercing rocks
and on the branches of the flowering trees
are thorns that thirst for blood.

UNREAL CITY

Driving over the bridge
under a tunnel of fog,
we face the lights of cars,
blurred, enlarged,
swimming, bobbing.

We'll never get out of here.
We are going on forever
unless we collide.

221

THIRTY BELOW

The prairie wind sounds colder
than any wind I have ever heard.
Looking through frosted windows
I see snow whirl in the street
and think how deep
all over the country now
snow drifts
and cars are stuck
on icy roads.
A solitary man walking
wraps his face in a woollen mask,
turns his back sometimes
so as not to front
this biting, eye-smarting wind.

Suddenly I see my dead father
in an old coat too thin for him,
the tabs of his cap pulled over his ears
on a drifted road in New Brunswick
walking with bowed head
towards home.

222

GOOD FRIDAY PERFORMANCE

The church is half-barn, half-forest.
Rafters stretch
in dim light, remote and branchlike.
The congregation rustles in.

Good Friday. Rain outside.
Umbrellas are parked dripping.
Here is shelter.
The choir will sing the Messiah.
We wait in ritual expectation.

Above in the branching rafters
a rustle, a flit of wings.
A child points. Another lifts her eyes.
"It's a bird."
"What is it?"
"It's a starling."
"It's a bird." "A starling."

Eyes turn, eyes gaze upward.
Flitting through branches,
perching on beams of the barn
in the dusty light,
the bird flies,
the mystery.

Who knows where it comes from
or where it goes to,
the bird that flies into the banquet hall
and out again?
If anyone can tell us news
of that bird
and its whereabouts,
we shall gladly listen.

This present bird, the starling,
cannot get out.
It flies up against the East Window,
the remote portrait of—is it?—Christ
and back again to a convenient beam.
It does not know what to do next.

"How will they ever get it out?
It's up too high for ladders."

The choir files in.
If its members see the bird,
they pay no attention.

It is a long afternoon.
All we like sheep...
We watch the bird.
He is resigned.
He is resting,
maybe listening.

The sparrow hath found a house...
Even thine altar...

The cross...
Suffering...
Lift up your heads, O ye gates.

Let him loose.
Let the caged spirit free.
The bird flits distractedly
here and there.
He cannot find the way.

Why do the kings of the earth rage
and the people imagine a vain thing?

The young man kneels,
head bowed, his children beside him.

He is angry.
War angers him.
The Lord will arise...

Behold, I show you a mystery.
We shall not all sleep...
We are back with you, bird,
confused, confined,
beating against the image,
caught between rafters and window.

Never mind, bird.
It's raining outside.
What would you do out there?
Better in here, in the barn
under the branches,
sheltering with mankind,
sheltering in the brave chorus
of hallelujahs.

Startled by the applause
you fly about wildly.
Be patient, be patient,
they will try to let you out

unless you fall first
crumpled, beaten, crazed,
the broken victim
on the altar

with the other Victim.

225

EASTER VIGIL

The dull day closes fine.
A last ray of sunshine warms
the sloped red roofs
the brown distant fields
still ridged with snow.

Tomorrow dawn will come again.
Gradually it will be spring.

In their graves the dead lie still.
The ground is cold
and heavy on their faces.
I am not so sure now
as I was once
that they will arise.

I am not sure
as I was once
that spring will always follow winter
that grass is inevitable,
dandelions, the cold smell of brooks
running.

Maybe we will all have to push
the round unwilling sun
like a huge wheel
so that it will rise again.

I wish I had a son
who built bridges
or a daughter who grew geraniums
in the kitchen window;
but if I did would they live forever?
Would the fountain of my blood
spring always in their veins?

Now in all the streets of the city
the lights are lit,
as the candles are lit
in the domed glowing church
below my window
to signify dawn
or the faith that dawn will come.

The dawn may not always come,
but tomorrow it will.
The blood will still flow
through my branched fingers.

See, with one finger
I touch a switch in my living room
and I too add my light
to all those others.

EASTER SUNDAY, QUAKER MEETING

I sit in a Quaker meeting
this Easter afternoon.
There are eight of us
on varnished chairs around a varnished table.
it is so still
I hear my neighbour's stomach rumble.
Another neighbour
begins to fall asleep.
I sit and daydream
of being in your arms.

Through stiff white curtains
the blue sunshine pours.
In the scrolled faded carpet
blue flowers twist in intricate patterns.
My eyes are on the floor
unless I raise them
to the shelf where someone has placed a flower pot
containing one ivy leaf.

Can the awaited Holy Spirit
console me for your absence?
Perhaps so.
I could put my head down now
on the flat varnished table
and fall asleep.
Or I could weep tears
of anguish, longing, desire, anger
for God

Or maybe you.

TO A FRIEND ON THE VERGE OF BREAKDOWN

Anguish has closed you in.
I walk round and round the glass walls
behind which you sit,
but find no entrance.
I too, I might say to you,
have known terror
and have survived it.
But, even if I could make you hear
through that thick transparent wall,
or if you could read my lips
as the deaf read them
when I try to mouth plainly,
how could I help you?

I have no wisdom
except that it is unwise
to trust wisdom,
that fear is more dangerous
than any danger,
that to be alive
means being in danger
and sometimes being unwise.

I cannot break the glass.
You must smash your own hand
through your own protection
and save yourself by blood.

FAMILY QUARREL: I

My brother struck my father
across the face
after a quarrel.
He was young, strong, and angry.

Afterwards my father cried aloud;
and, watching the tears fall
from his pale blue eyes,
wiped off by his hand,
I felt as though
God had been struck
and was weeping.

FAMILY QUARREL: II

My father, being bitter against my sister,
cried out, "That my own daughter
should run the roads, and make love in ditches
like a common drab!"

BLUEFLAG

So that I would not pick the blueflag
in the midst of the pond
(and get my clothes wet)
my mother told me that it was poison.

I watched this beautiful, frightening flower
growing up from the water
from its green reeds,
washed blue, sunveined,
and wanted it more
than all the flowers I was allowed to pick,
wild roses, pink and smooth as soap,
or the milk-thin daisies
with butterblob centres.

I noticed that the midges
that covered the surface of the water
were not poisoned by the blueflag,
but I thought they must have
a different kind of life from mine.

Even now, if I pick one,
fear comes over me, a trembling.
I half expect to be struck dead
by the flower's magic

a potency seeping
from its dangerous blue skin
its veined centre.

INHERITANCE

I

As a child I overheard my deaf father
talking to himself, wondering
where the next meal was coming from, saying
"All's lost," saying
"What will we do?"
Saying, "They'd be better off without me."

And I followed him about dumbly,
wishing to say "I love you"
fearing where he might walk
or what he might do
wishing to make him successful
brilliant and admired,

and not this shabby man
with mended trousers
and scuffed shoes
stumbling apologetically about the house.

2

He was a good man, my father,
a childlike man,
never given to violence, afraid of blood,
afraid of hurting others, a gentle man;
yet I think I was ashamed of him a little
because he never won in life,
also because he tried to comfort himself
by pretending to despise those who prospered,
and because he talked too loudly
and repeated the same jokes many times.

But I could never cut him out of myself,
my argumentative, mild father,
arrogant and timid.

Sometimes lately
I find I also repeat the same jokes.

3

My mother was always hunting for four-leaf clovers,
and, since her eyes were quick, she found many.
They were stuffed in all her books and Bibles,
but she complained to me once
that they did not bring her luck.

I repeated her words to a neighbour
and she rebuked me later.

"Never tell anyone outside the family"
she warned me then,
"that any of us don't think we are lucky."

4

Green was my mother's favourite colour,
colour of grass and hope.
All her life she wanted
a green velvet dress
and never had one.

BRIDGE

I remember walking the bridge across the river
one evening in spring with my mother
when I was thirteen.
We took turns carrying a suitcase
which had in it just about all we owned,
and we were not sure with which relatives
we might spend the night.
It was a high, clear evening,
with the new moon out and all the stars,
and we stopped halfway over the bridge
to look down into the quiet water
so still and so deep.

I thought my mother,
who liked beautiful things,
was only admiring the stars
reflected;
but now I know
she must have been thinking
how peaceful it would be
down there
far below the bridge.

234

LAST NIGHT

Last night
I talked to myself in the library stacks.
I was a schoolgirl
with long hair.
I wore cotton stockings
and a plaid jumper
I had sewn for myself.

I was very ambitious.
I intended to learn
everything.

235

COLD TEA

The old woman is dying gradually
in the spare bedroom of the farmhouse.
She is waited on
by her unwilling daughter-in-law
and by an occasional grandchild
wandering into the room
between games of school or store
or blindman's buff.

On her bedside table
her black Bible rests
between a liniment bottle
and a glass of water
beginning to fill with air bubbles.

She would like to pour me
a cup of tea
but the pot on the dresser
has gone cold.

236

THE OLD MAN

The old man
walking to the village post office
walks carefully,
knowing his bones are brittle
knowing that walking too fast
getting excited
getting annoyed
might bring on
his final stroke.

He carries his wife's letter
to their son,
hopes there will be something in return.

His eyes, now far sighted,
miss the pebbles at his feet,
but see distant hills.
He is too deaf to hear
what the children say,
playing on the sidewalk,
almost knocking into him with their bicycles.
It is almost not worth while
to have lived to be so old:
except that the sun shines
warms the ache
of his cold bones.

ABE

I rather admired old Abe MacNeill
and his long Presbyterian prayers
every night after supper.
I thought he must be devout
because he said so.

But my mother said,
"Look at what he pays his hired man
and how his wife and daughter
are bowed down with work
and never smile at all."

EASTER VACATION

I meet my friend from Hong Kong
who reminds me
of the time twenty years ago when we drove,
seven of us, up into the Lake District—
two Chinese, four East Indians, one Canadian—
and invoked the ghost of William Wordsworth
among the rocks of Cumberland.

All those daffodils
wet
she remembers,
and the hikers carrying knapsacks,
and rain on Windermere,
and Hawkshead Schoolhouse,
where old William had played.

Also, the cold hotel
where we talked all night
four in a room,
taking turns putting pennies in the gas meter,
and our worries about
our vegetarian Hindu friend
who we thought might starve;
and the other who could not do
without her tea
at exactly the right
inconvenient time.

And we came back to London
almost not speaking to one another
but singing on the way
to keep our spirits up
a Hindi love song,
O Canada, and
It's a long long way to Tipperary.

239

SUMMER TIME

I remember a week in Wales
in an old house
where I read through afternoons of rainy weather
George Borrow writing of Wales and Spain.

Outside were tall hills
and a squelching walk through wet grass
to a small grey castle
bleak and military
where there was nothing really to see

and inside at tea my host argued
in a singing Welsh voice
in favour of vegetarianism
which he saw as the hope of the world.

My room was narrow
lit at night by my bedside candle.
From its one window
I saw the village church.
The wet summer wind
blew the white curtains.

I lay in the hard bed
with my mind turning round and round
my future.
I was sailing home to Canada next month
and did not want to go.

BLOCK OF SILENCE

No, I shall never return. That fact is certain.
The farewell hand-wave, and the answering smile
Seen crookedly, as though through depths of waves—
This is the definite and abrupt conclusion.
Never again beside the evening Thames
Or on a bus top in the afternoon fog
Shall we seek solitude in the crowded city;
Never sit arguing over muddy coffee
In dingy cafeterias; never stop
For violets and daffodils at the corner stalls.

I could not ever come back to sit beside you
And find the air frozen to ice between us
So that meanings are not heard, and words become
Pick-axes chipping at the block of silence.
I will not be a ghost returned to plague you.
I will not hurt you, or let you hurt me
By any casual, unintentional change.
I will not let this Thames, like other rivers,
Withdraw into a beauty strange and hard,
Grown to a metal smoothness in the sun.

It is better to cut off hope in the beginning.
The lips one kisses goodbye on the station platform
Accustom themselves to other lips and eyes,
Are only embarrassed by former intimacies;
And if I save myself I save you too.
No, I shall not return, and you will not be sorry.

VOYAGE HOME

Seasick on the Atlantic
drinking ginger ale
looking through the porthole
at greygreen sea;

or recovered, walking
the deck in August
dressed for winter,
watching the distant
icebergs floating
or the sunsets
orange
burning;

or later, in the St. Lawrence,
sitting in a deck chair,
wrapped in sun and checked blanket,
as villages slid past
white and decorous
with their tall churches;

I was coming home
to the high blue sky
to the Montreal station
with its park outside
to the creaking train
wheezing all night
through towns in New England;
to breakfast in the diner
with ice water cold on tongue,
as I watched the hot bleached fields
through the dirty window;

to the last stretch
of summer woods,
to my parents standing
older than I remembered
on the station platform
in the wooden town;

to a future I could not see
and hoped for
and feared,

far from the city
where the week before
I had waked in my stripped room
and said goodbye
to the square outside
and all the shabby, loved
Bloomsbury streets.

It was the summer
the Korean War started
and Mackenzie King died.

Others beside me
walked the deck
or looked out the train window,
counting time
as water, clouds, grass
rushed to meet them
with a question.

CHRISTMAS DAY: ROAD TO OBAN

Driving a snowy road towards Oban
I think of the homesick Scots of the world
and understand both why they leave home
and why they are homesick.

This landscape haunts dreams;
and the closed eye sees
rocks, hills, water, bending roads,
sheep on the roads, a flight of birds,
a few sparse trees
remote from houses
in a veil of snow.

Caesar did not conquer here,
nor the English really.
A stubborn, Northern land,
difficult to come by,
I can imagine it still
when H-bombs have wrecked other countries
sheltering a rugged soul or two
in its borders
and a few birds and sheep.

244

NEW YEAR'S EVE

I remember you twenty or so years ago
when I first saw you,
a plain young man, awkward and bony,
thick-lipped, coarse-haired,
with nothing attractive but your eyes;
and I remember making fun of you for your clowning
and because you were too eager to be liked.
I remember quarrelling with you and wanting to tease you;
and I think with tenderness
of that young man,
gentle, coarse, wistful, and a little silly,
whom I now realize
I must have loved
with the perverse and inarticulate passion
of one terrified of loving
and therefore wanting to torment
you and myself.

Now, in this room full of people,
while New Year's Eve is draining away,
we talk to each other in a corner
over another person's head;
and the ghosts of those absurd young people
come back to haunt the room,
so that I do not know
how much this ache of desire
is for you as you are now
sitting here in the tree-lit room
quoting Yeats to me
and how much is for
the young man you once were,
exuberant, gay and quarrelsome.

But I feel, as I watch you
turn the glass in your hand,
a wish like a sudden pain,
regardless of past or present,
to be held so tight in your arms
I could never escape
but die to myself and to time
and be one flesh with you forever.

I THOUGHT OF YOU

I thought of you whom once I thought I loved.
Your silent ghost stood by me in the room,
and smiled, and said, "What are you thinking of?"
I looked, and looked, and felt my throat go dumb.

"Nothing," I said, and saw your eyes go down
my throat and past my breast. I tried to say
"You're well? When did you come?"
Your eyes caught mine, and held, then turned away.

You pulled a chair towards me and sat down.
Through summer windows summer daylight streamed.
The room was full of people, but they seemed
distant and strange as clouds, silent as stone,
unreal as actors waiting for a cue.
I touched your hand, and knew you were not you.

246

A NEW OLD SONG

Those whom I loved, I love no more;
those who loved me no more love me.
I'll be like that miller of ancient times
who lived beside the river Dee.

I'll sing a song, a happy song.
Why should I need your company?
Last winter's snow will soon be gone
and new leaves come on the leafless tree.

I'll buy fresh tulips for my room,
red petals streaked with lines of white.
I'll buy a book of poetry
and read it for my own delight.

I'll pour red wine into a glass
and drink a toast to myself alone.
I'll say to the silly world, Go by,
Go by, you lifeless ball of stone;

I never loved you much, and now
I like you less as each day goes by;
I wash my hands of your blood and sands,
and say, You silly world, goodbye.

247

SHOCK

The world skidded, but I stood stock still,
frozen to marble on the marble stair,
while all about me in layers of cold stone
fell the stiff folds of the sculptured air.

I split from myself like a husk, was blown as light
as a queen from a pack of cards, on cardboard feet,
till, reaching the window, I suddenly saw myself
diminishing down the length of the bleak street.

TWEEZERS

Carefully
with my tweezers
I remove
one small hair
from the nipple
of my breast.

Perhaps you might
cross all these miles
arrive unannounced
and discover
this imperfection.

248

REMEMBERING THIS BLISS

Remembering
how my hands stroked your face
your cheeks hot on my cool palms
my fingers moving
lightly over your eyebrows
and only just grazing
your warm mouth.

Remembering
holding in my lap
your skull full of dreams
your breathing body
the strange remoteness
close.

Remembering
your kisses on my breasts
my nipples trembling
laughter breaking
from my throat

Remembering
this bliss.

POEMS FOR PSYCHOANALYSIS

PSYCHOANALYST

The psychoanalyst has a German accent,
is over sixty but has dyed her hair,
wears an ornate brooch
to fasten her ruffled blouse.

She loses her temper easily,
yet her patients love her
days when they don't hate her.
The alcoholic, the drug addict, the homosexual,
the woman who never wears any colour but white
and never takes her gloves off
for fear of germs on her fingers—
they all love her indiscriminately
and hate her indiscriminately
with a love and a hate which is not really for her.

Is the psychoanalyst herself neurotic
to need all this love and hate?
I don't know; it is hard for a patient to tell.

DIARIES

The patient dreams
of standing in water
on which diaries are floating.
He pushes them under
the layers of water
but they rise again
floating like cork
and will not be submerged.

EXPLORER

He dreams
of discovering a large egg
labelled "Newfoundland."
When he cracks the shell
he will be able to walk in
and find himself at the centre.

CHILDHOOD INNOCENCE

When the analyst's nephew died
the patients all said they were sorry
but were really glad
because there was one less person
to share her with.
Little children dance
(even though they love him)
at the thought of their brother's funeral.

251

Her commonest dream is one
of being smothered or else strangled.
Stiff in her bed,
she hears footsteps approach.
A stealthy, violent figure
bends above her,
Othello or the Boston Strangler.
She struggles for life
as though, waking and finding it not a dream,
she must turn her own fingers against
the foreign throat;
then finds the strangler is her mother,
screams "I must live," and this time really wakes
in the sweating sheets
wondering if anyone heard
her screamed whispered cry.

OUT OF THE DEPTHS

I have fallen down a dark spinning space
into a depth of dreams.
I walk about under water.
It is all ripples.
My head hurts
down here.
My head expands to hold
the roar of waters,
the humming of deafness
in my ears.

DREAM

I dance naked before the king,
whose throne is built on the sea shore
and who looks
remarkably like everyone I ever loved.

But though my thighs are of snow
and my gold hair sets fire to the world
as it blows in the wind of my dancing
I do not satisfy the king.

He will never give me
John the Baptist's head.
I shall never touch
those beautiful murdered eyes.

WHEN I GO TO SLEEP

I think
when I go to sleep
that I will dream
of golden apples and green winds

But I dream of dusty roads
and pigsties
and a shabby
deserted
merry-go-round.

GAMES IN AN INSTITUTION

I carry my heart in my hand
in a pink plastic box.
The floor is slippery and slopes upward.
I am afraid I may drop my heart
in the midst of the crowd,
but I do not think it will break.
It is made of durable material
and may perhaps bounce.

We plan to play games with our hearts.
We have all lined up
outside a box office
in order to get our hockey sticks.

The woman standing beside me
decides to take off her clothes.
She makes faces at us.
We ignore her, as politely as we can,
and someone says, "Poor soul, she can't help it.
She'll be as sensible as can be
tomorrow."

A few people slide on the polished floor.
Somehow, however, no one
ever gets around to playing games.

ANSWER

In my dream
I spoke to you.
"Give me pain," I cried.
"Give me terror. Only be."

I was on my knees.
I was a child in a white nightgown
drinking a cup of tears.

When I awoke
pain from neck to foot
broke over my body.

ON EL GRECO'S PAINTING OF THE AGONY IN THE GARDEN

This Christ is young.
He has Spanish eyes.
A lady might think of him
as her lover
kneeling with ardent devotion,
an upward gaze.
He might be inventing
a sonnet
to an unapproachable virgin
whom he wished to approach.

255

His hands, however, are not lover's hands.
The skeleton beneath is too visible.
His fingers are like branches,
white and graceful.
He is dressed in red
for blood
for martyrdom
and kneels on blue.

Behind him the stone is sharp.
Bushes are thin and bare.
A white moon
slides behind gauze.
To one side
the gauzy night
enfolds his sleeping friends.

Above him leans the angel
with sharp wings
who holds the golden
heavy cup.

The night is long.
Those who betray him draw near.

256

FOR A DEAD TEACHER

We all laughed at you, funny man—
sometimes laughed with you—
you with your pet goats,
your ten-year-old hats,
your love of loud drinking songs.

If we did not laugh, you told us
"I will put up a sign, saying,
'Laugh, please: joke.'"

You raged at us for being stupid,
conventional, nice boys and girls
who would age into I.O.D.E. faces
or business paunches.

"Broaden your minds, folks,"
you cried,
"Broaden your minds,"
as we sat quietly doodling in our note books,
drawing pictures of goats.

Old teacher, old clown,
how did we fail to see
with what sadness
you told all your jokes?

RECOGNITION

After a dozen years, I see a friend
who was once beautiful, with a sculptured head
like Nefertiti, her dark hair braided
in lapidary coils,
her eyes green and liquid as cat's eyes;
and I find myself gazing too hard
at the marks of time and weather
even a monument acquires.

I too have crow's feet;
my hair too grows grey beneath the dye;
the nose, with the passage of time, becomes more beaked.
But I was always a plain girl.
Beauty so cut from stone, I think,
should be more durable.

And yet I admire this tall, gaunt woman,
walking proudly with her wrinkles,
whose eyes are no longer cat's eyes
but the eyes of an eagle
staring from a high mountain
at wide worlds below.

HE RETURNS TO THE HOUSE
WHERE HE WAS BORN

Coming back, after many years,
with his car and children,
he drives slowly, wondering if he has missed the house.
The landmarks seem in the wrong places:
the covered bridge, the general store, the churches,
the school (now deserted) where they stop and peer
through windows at the piles of ancient school books
gathering dust.
The road is lonelier even than in the old days
with more abandoned houses,
barns with their roofs caved in.

He knows now he must have passed the house,
goes back,
and sees it finally
half-hidden in trees,
no path through the bush to it,
sagging, paintless,
its windows boarded up.

He is surprised
the house is smaller than he thought it was.

A neighbour tells him
a millionaire from Florida has bought it,
will clear the land and build a summer house—
or so they say; he doesn't much believe them.

Tonight he will dream
the house alive again,
the lake behind it
rippled and dark
in the summer evening
or turned to ice
on which children fly
with screams like birds.

ROUND TRIP

I

I try to climb up the stairway
and into the house again,
but the space between the steps
has grown too wide.
I cannot make it.

So I call to my mother
that I am leaving
and walk down the hill
towards the river.
It is the dark hour before
sunrise, with no stars.
I am sure I shall lose the path,
blinded in woods,
but miraculously
I find the way.

2

I come to a park
before a mansion
extravagantly Tudor.
The weather is May.
Sun shines on wet grass.
Everybody lies on grass,
ladies in long green dresses
light as foam
with jewelled hair falling
down white shoulders,
and golden-bearded men
laughing at their jokes.
A band plays military music.
It is picnic weather,
everybody's holiday,
but I cannot stay.

3

I walk through an exhibition
of paintings, mostly portraits
dusky coloured, in heavy frames,
women with long ringed hands
holding fans
before anonymous faces,
men with the pride and grossness
of power and wealth in their eyes.

Also there is a room for showing
various instruments of torture.

261

4

Now it is June.
We have come by motorboat on the river.
We are lost in the maze,
and call to each other over the hedges
laughing because we know
we shall not be lost long.
We shall eat strawberries and cream
afterwards in the garden
under a striped awning.

There is almost no night
in June.

5

In a square classroom
with a pointer in my hand
I stand explaining my dream.
There is a blackboard
on which I make notes
with white chalk.
My explanation satisfies others
but not myself.

6

I have come back.
I walk on a hill
as on a lookout.
I can see for miles.
I intend to install a telescope
through which I can see
men landing on the moon.

I am not sure
whether it is good or bad
to have come home again

or if I intend to stay.

263

GATREY KETCHESON

The youngest Ketcheson girl, six years old
in the fall of 1820,
walking between her father's and her sister's
in the country near Sydney,
strayed into the woods and was lost.
For nine days, including eight nights,
the neighbours searched for her
with barking dogs.
All the nights were cold
and two were rainy.

Barefoot and shivering
in her thin jacket,
she wandered under pines,
the notched brown bracken
wet beneath her feet.
She nibbled at wintergreen
leaves and berries.
Once a pitying bird
dropped down an acorn
into her lap,
but she would not eat it,
thinking it belonged
to the young birds.

Far off in the farmyards
she could hear the cocks crow
in the early morning
and the dinner horn at noon
calling the men to eat;
but she lost the sounds' direction,
stumbling over branches.

Once she came out into a clearing
near a cabin
but she thought it belonged to Indians
and ran away frightened
remembering strange stories.

One night she slept
under a spruce tree
her head on a stump.
One night when it rained
she crawled into
a hollow log.
One night a strange grey animal
crept to her feet
and kept her warm.
She was glad of the warmth
but afraid to breathe
for fear he would kill her.

On the ninth day
she lay down early in the afternoon,
saying her prayers
as she had been taught.

Then the men found her
and carried her off,
and handed her to her mother
with great rejoicing.

MUNCHAUSEN IN ALBERTA

Our first winter in the settlement,
the old man said,
January was so cold
the flames in the lamp froze.
The womenfolk picked them like strawberries
and gave them to the children to eat.

That's the only time
I was ever a fire-eater.

ANOTHER SUNRISE: OCTOBER 18, 1970

I awake to the usual morning,
a cloudy day, the sky grieved and yellowish,
and my usual concerns are with me,
disappointments, desires, ambitions.

But I do not lament today my private losses.
I lament for my country,
the good, dull country into which I was born,
which I have slighted.

And where has it gone, my dull, empty country,
with its winds across endless space,
with its kind, boring people
who worked between Sunday sermon and Saturday movie,
whose complaints were muted, whose politics were colourless?
A puritanical people, a self-righteous people
without much love for poetry,
earnest, hard working, glum,
violent only at hockey.

I would like them back.

I would call them from the dead
to stand on guard O Canada
for their children who have lost the strength,
who have lost the necessary dullness.

I look out my window at the coloured roof tops
under the heavy sky.
A few cars pass,
two orange busses.
The day
looks peaceful.
Maybe the Second Coming
will be delayed another week.

I intend to go for a walk, I intend
to turn off my transistor.
Maybe we shall yet build Jerusalem
in the true north.

267

MINOR DISAGREEMENT

You tell me over the telephone
that poetry is always celebration;
but I disagree, remembering
Hopkins crying
"I am gall, I am heartburn,"
remembering Coleridge writing
out of his despondency,
his life without hope;
remembering Shelley dejected near Naples,
Cowper perishing
"whelm'd in deeper gulfs"
than any castaway.

The poet writes
sometimes in joy
but sometimes lamenting
the sick rose
the dead groundhog
dead soldiers, the Great Duke,
the seasons that return but do not bring
the lost sight, the lost
familiar faces, the faded
daffodils, chrysanthemums;

lamenting all beautiful, proud, living, gone
things.

Sometimes the poet,
"half in love with easeful death,"
demands to be hurt,
asks for pain, likes
"a look of agony,"
preaches in his shroud.

The poet is not
wiser, better, gayer
than housewives, business men, union leaders
or politicians.

All he has
is language
to express
joy, grief, aloneness,
the tears of the world,
its fires, tempests, tigers,

the snow falling
on the old woman out for a walk.

FOG

The morning is foggy.
Cars drive silently to work.
A woman walks through snow
a coat without a face.

It will be difficult this morning
to manage to see the sun rise.

269

POETRY FOR BREAKFAST

"The true poet is willing to give up poetry in order to find
poetry."—Henry Rago, *Poetry*, August 1967, p. 336.

I am reading poetry magazines for breakfast
and, because I am a slow reader, they are out of date,
but some dateless, about love or suicide
or northern lights
or maybe lemon trees.

People travel. They look through windows. They are bored.
They keep bees.
Sometimes they go mad.
Don't you know there's a war on?
At the edge of Liberal, Kansas,
something, maybe the grass, is whispering.
There is a Breathing Lesson.
There are even sonnets, though not many.

Some of the names are familiar. I see them
going through several marriages.
Some of them turn up once: it is the year
they took that course at Bread Loaf.

Why do they all write, I wonder?
Why do they not take snapshots
of the Vicks VapoRub Factory
or the girl under the lemon tree?
or cut the obituary out of yesterday's paper?

I make myself another pot of tea.
The morning dazzles,
this last day of October.
I think our latest snow
may last the winter.

GOLD MAN

I sit in my chair
with my hands and head full
of other people's poems.
Do I need to write too?

I drink rum and hot water
and am sleepy.
In my head a chant runs on
said by the gold man
about children and chains of gold.

No, I cannot chant too.

I come from a country
of slow and diffident words
of broken rhythms
of unsaid feelings.

Next time I am born
I intend to come
from a different country.

271

FESTIVAL OF RELIGION AND THE ARTS

At the front of the room
the young bearded man
reads an old Buddhist poet.
The poet, like St. Francis,
had loved Lady Poverty,
lived with simplicity
in a hut on the side of a mountain.

Upwards the young faces
yearn towards light.

I remember sitting, aged twenty-five,
in a Chicago railway station
reading Thomas Merton.
At the other end of the hard bench
sat a middle-aged negro mother
with her baby
who would now, I think, be grown up.
Round us a crowd whirled
men women children
everyone in a hurry
killing time.

Could one withdraw,
could one find illumination
away from the crowds
and the baby
    (who needed his diaper changed)?
Could one illuminate
find holiness in
crowd and baby, fat black woman
with fallen arches?

When I was nineteen I had no illusions
or had the illusion I had none.

Since then I have gained an illusion every year
and lost it the year after.
Now I think I might after all
dust off my Greek dictionary
read a few choruses from Sophocles.

I might take up bird watching.
I might even live in a shack
on the side of a mountain,
except that I would like
to be near a Safeway or a Loblaws
and I do not like mice.

Buddhists, I take it,
do not like traps.

Quakers are quarrelsome. In the True Church
Gregorian chant has been replaced by Methodist hymns.
Where can I go?

Thou hast the words....

The young man from Glasgow
reads a poem about Incarnation.
A painful, possibly a ludicrous
Dogma. Maybe true.

273

I watch with pity the young faces.
They are not my flesh,
but they continue me.
I wish them better luck than I had,
or than their parents had,
but I doubt if they will get it.

Unto us a Child is born.

ON WINTER'S LONGEST NIGHT

On winter's longest night
we drive through shadowed streets.
The pines are lit with blue.
A Santa Claus revolves
on a white lawn.

On winter's darkest night
the fiery Christmas lights
are lit to bring the sun
back from his bed,
while icy stars revolve
electric in the sky.

On winter's longest street
the swinging signboards shine
and scrolls and letters spell
a greeting for the sun.

YEAR'S END

On this pitchblack morning
of the last week in December
I sit by the train window
eating toast and jam,
trying to see out.

At Wainwright
there are lights in houses,
an electric Christmas wreath
flashing red and blue
from the front of the station.

Gradually shapes appear
buildings slide past.
The new snow is grey-green
in the half light.

Near the town of Viking
we sway past a dump
where cars and trucks
lie on their sides
half-filled with snow.
A pile of tires,
a clump of green tractors
lie under drifts.

275

Under the pale sky
the snow is washed with light,
becomes blue
tinged with the faint pink
of the unseen sunrise.
Trees are like artificial trees
made of handkerchiefs.
In some fields the snow is ridged
becomes goose pimpled.
Brown grass stubbles the white.

Far off in one field
a red-brown horse moves
warm in the whiteness.
There is a red barn with a blue roof
there there
and there
is a black dog running.

276

SUNDAY EVENING, FEBRUARY

In my rectangular apartment
interchangeable
in a highrise
in a provincial city
I stand in my kitchen
about to make tea.
My open novel
has fallen to the floor.

I might have lived in Bombay,
I think.
I might have lived in London
in a small flat
reading the same novel
a year or so earlier,
taking it to work with me
to read on the tube,

Or somewhere in New Brunswick
back woods, married to the farm boy
from next door, now middle-aged,
I might have been calculating,
How do we get the kids through high school?

It is not too late.
I can still choose
Wellington or Dublin.
I can still go to Athens
in hot weather.

277

But it is not place,
I think.
It is not another place
I need.
This one will do.
It is full of strangeness,
it is full of other people.

Ah, if I could watch them
without their watching me,
if I could lift the roofs from all the highrises
so that I could see them
in the absurdity of their love,
in their quarrels,
or sitting at kitchen tables
nervously drinking tea or beer.

I will drink my tea clear
in a white cup
without a pattern.

278

HOW TO KEEP WARM

Days grow longer.
Snow slides off the roofs.
Outside my office window
a dozen cedar waxwings
perch in one small bush.

Birds keep warm in a cold climate
because feathers are warmer than fur
and also because
(so the book I am reading says)
it takes more energy to
fly than just to plod
bearlike or manlike
over the snow.

279

MARCH AFTERNOON

Suddenly it is spring
and cars come splashing
rivers of mud and water
while people walking leap
over rippling puddles,
balance on ice and slime.

Brown snow melts,
mixed with candy wrappers,
last year's leaves,
cigarette butts
and crushed red berries,

and overhead the sky
softens
is a paler blue
tepid
where one cloud floats.

Coats are unbuttoned,
scarves thrust into pockets,
and there—one girl who abandoned
rubber boots too early
picks her way delicately
over the small islands of mud
and ice.

MOVING DAY AGAIN

It is time to move again
to discard all these dresses
of the wrong length, the year-before-last boots,
letters, old magazines, unfinished poems.

There are scratches on the furniture.
The television no longer works.
I am tired of the view.

Shall I live on Fogo Island,
or in Vancouver,
or somewhere in the sky-filled prairie?

Tell me.
I pull a fresh card from the pack.
What does it mean?

I am advertising for a new
magician. The old one
is repeating himself.

281

UNDER A PLANE TREE

I read (this cold blizzardy morning
with gusts of snow blowing
outside my window)
of you, Socrates, under a plane tree
on the banks of the Ilissus
talking of love and rhetoric
in hot Greek weather.

(They have walked through grass
    these friends
    taking off their sandals
    by the brook.
    Grasshoppers sing
    the lovers of the Muses
    who never thirst or hunger
    but sing always.
    It would be easy
    to fall asleep
    instead of talking
    even about love.)

I too could sleep
blanket wrapped around me
watching snow fall
imagining the spot outside Athens.

But I turn the page to read
(once more, old friend and teacher)
of your death,
the poisoned cup
drained with dignity,
the weeping friends
forbidden to weep.

"No evil can happen to a good man
either in life or after death."

Ah, yes, again you prove
(doubt though I often may)
that love and language conquer death.

283

UNDERSEA GARDENS

The diver, in the underwater gardens,
moves like a fish with flippered feet.
Bubbles rise from him.
He waves his hand to children behind glass
or carries carefully for them to see
the huge dangerous octopus
many tentacled
or the small comic prickly sea urchin.

Fish eat from his hand.
Look at them come like birds or puppies
called for their dinner.
The sea cucumber beneath his stroking
swells like a small balloon.
He has returned for this brief space of time
to the old world we came from
green and liquid.
Around him sail our brothers
perch and greenling
with wide cold eyes.
Their blood is cold and slow.
Enviously, we watch behind glass
our dangerous past
which we cannot revisit.

The children and their mothers
clap and cheer.

284

DAYSPRING

Can the world recover
the innocence of white birches?
Can water be washed?
Can fire consume itself
and grow grass from its ashes?

Each morning
out of the east
comes a strong man riding.
His horse's eyes are coals
and its mane is smoke.
He has always come
even when he has not been greeted.

O god of morning
who has never before failed your children
whom you drew up out of the slime and ooze

save   save.

285

ALCHEMIST

Man, the evil magician,
brews, in the perishable cauldron
of rock and sand,
a violent, fiery potion,
melted lightning.

Foolish enchanter,
do not break
this great brown dish
with green edges
which has been in the family
all these years.
Where will you find another
to hold your children's supper?

286

ADVICE TO THE FEARFUL SELF

If necessary, go through madness.
If necessary, walk through a wall of fire.
Let the flames eat your hand.
Let your body shrivel like the top of a burnt match stick.

If necessary, drown.
Walk undersea like the deepsea diver
but without his mask or oxygen supply.
Let the waves close over you.
See above your head
the webbed feet of seabirds
flying in water.

If necessary, be buried live.
Let sand clog your nostrils.
Close your mouth on pebbles.
In the frozen ground
stiffen with winter.

If necessary, be conceived again.
Swim in the river of the womb
till, cast up fishlike on dry land
you grow a mouth and scream.

If necessary, scream.

ELIZABETH BREWSTER was born in New Brunswick, but since 1972 has lived in Saskatoon, where she is now Professor Emeritus at the University of Saskatchewan. She has published five books of fiction, two volumes of autobiography and nineteen collections of poetry. An earlier collection, *Footnotes to the Book of Job*, was shortlisted for the Governor General's Award. She has been awarded an honorary doctorate by the University of New Brunswick, the E.J. Pratt Award and the President's Medal, as well as the Saskatchewan Lifetime Achievement Award. In the last two years she has turned eighty years of age, converted to Judaism and become a member of the Order of Canada.